Joanna Thornhill
Foreword by Michelle Ogundehin

INTERIOR DESIGN MASTERS

a practical guide to
decorating your home

Hardie Grant

QUADRILLE

CONTENTS

Chapter 5
Design styles and signature styels 116

Chapter 6
Sourcing and customising 178

Chapter 7
The finishing touches 202

Foreword

People often ask me what makes a great interior designer. My answer is always the same: curiosity, enthusiasm and empathy for the user, alongside, quite simply, the desire to make the world a more beautiful, if not healing, place to be, one space at a time.

But interior design mastery is also about that incredibly abstract thing, intuition. I attempt to define this as the ability to decipher a space in all its tangible dimensions — aspect, light, volume, heritage, location — as well as the people who will use it. The purpose being to create something that is designed and decorated to fit that user in all the right places with the comfort and individuality of a custom-made jacket.

And this isn't easy! It comes from developing a sense for reading a room to understand what it needs; the talent to pull together colour, finishes and furnishings to create an ambience that affects how you feel; and most crucially, it's about exceeding expectations to give a client something that they often didn't know they needed, or wanted. Add this all together and you start to understand why some liken the role of the designer to that of a skilled psychotherapist!

It's also incredibly important. After all, we shape our environments and thereafter our environments shape us, so it behoves the designer to recognise this power, and to use it wisely. In short, I like to think of interior design as a process of painting pictures of possibility so that people can begin to dream of what a space could be, and most importantly, who they could thus become in that space.

Bottom line, interior design is a path to enabling our best selves. And what could be more rewarding, or exciting, than that.

Michelle Ogundehin

About this book

As a nation, us Brits are somewhat obsessed with interior design (both improving our own and eyeing up what our peers or the professionals are up to). And, as Interior Design Masters shows, restyling and rejuvenating our spaces offers more than merely surface-deep improvements: it can teach us new skills, help us think more creatively and even enhance our feelings of happiness when we finally achieve an end result that feels like home.

But design success is about more than simply having a brilliant eye for interiors: as each design contestant (40 and counting) featured across the series has discovered, the magic is just as often found within the mistakes and mishaps as it is in perfectly planned and executed schemes. That ability to think on your feet and course-correct as and when things go wrong, or when tight timeframes necessitate a spur-of-the-moment rejig, is just as important as practical know-how and possessing an instinctive sense of style - and it's a skill you can hone, too.

This book aims to demystify the world of interior design, and help you harness your own innate interior design mastery (for it is there, within all of us), whether you're playing with ideas in a rental, or a homeowner looking to get a bit more hands-on and creative with your renovations.

Designed to work as a standalone tome, it leans heavily on the ethos and guiding principles of the series, though whether you're a die-hard fan or simply looking for some sound design advice, there is plenty of insight and inspiration to take away. Alongside an easy-to-follow framework, these pages share guidance from the many voices who contributed to the show, from the design authority of its expert guest judges and the practical advice of its on-screen tradespeople, to tips and insights from the design contestants themselves sharing first-hand their learnings and lightbulb moments.

Illustrations throughout are based on many of the design schemes and projects created by these aspiring designers, revisiting some of the show's most successful spaces and exploring in greater detail what made them so memorable as well as unpacking examples of their signature styles. With insights into why they work, and how you can recreate key aspects of each design in your own home, it encourages you to learn from these projects, yet give them your own unique spin to suit your home and aesthetic.

Most importantly, however, these pages contain the overriding Interior Design Masters DNA: the advice given throughout is wholly practical and designed to adapt

Want to see more from the design contestants and judges who made each show so memorable? Turn to pages 252-253 to find their websites and social bio's, many of which contain extra behind-the-scenes content and snippets from the show as well as detailing their various post-show project work. And if you'd like to check out any of the previous series, they are available on BBC iPlayer.

and apply to any situation, enabling you to create a home that *feels* like you - all while offering many actionable tips and ideas to help you create it. Yes, there are some rules to follow (alongside ways to twist and bend them to best suit your specific needs), but often the secret sauce comes when a budding designer develops the confidence and clarity in their own visions and ability, enabling them to create something with an authenticity and - as Michelle Ogundehin would say - that all-important sense of signature style.

These pages will talk you through the key aspects you need to know in order to learn how to speak your own personal design language, such as:

- Understanding your signature style, and how you can use this to inform all your design decisions.
- Practical steps to take when planning your project, from honing your design ideas to creating a budget and organising your order of works.
- Key design principles, broken down by room, detailing the most effective layouts and furniture for that given space.

- The fundamental elements required for the success of any scheme, from how to use lighting to create ambiance, to accessorising a space using tried-and-trusted styling rules.
- Ways to shop sustainably and incorporate planet-friendly furniture and accessories within your home - and why this is so important.

As well as in-depth case studies from completed spaces across the series, there are also detailed how-to's, from lampshade hacks to how you can create your own box seating from scratch, with advice on how to either copy what you've seen on screen or create your own bespoke variations.

Whether you're looking to make the most of a small space or create a jaw-dropping statement room, this book will be an invaluable catalyst for unleashing your creative vision, and mastering your own interiors.

1

An introduction to interiors

'It's one thing creating a flat vignette, as we often see on our Instagram squares, or a highly stylised space manicured for a magazine front cover, but it's a totally different ballgame working on the three dimensions of a physical space to live in. It's always a good idea to understand the room's end-use and consider the practical elements of how a space needs to work for you as well as all the design details. I always start any space with the floor first, then the big-ticket, larger items and the lighting, and I leave all the details and accessory sourcing to the very end. Much like when painting a canvas, you usually sketch out the background first, then the mid-ground, before moving on to the foreground details.'

Matthew Williamson, *Interior Designer and Guest Judge*

where to begin?

Whether you've never decorated before or are a seasoned home improver, it's often daunting trying to determine where to begin. It can be all too easy to get caught in the trap of simply copying a look you've spotted in a magazine, or impulsively ordering a piece of furniture or paint colour then feeling stuck as to how to use it.

As with most things in life, groundwork is key, so before you pick up a paint brush or start an online shopping spree, take a step back and try to drill down into what you really want – which can sometimes be very different from what's caught your eye when scrolling through Instagram.

As tempting as it can be to delve head-first into designing (aka the fun bit!), to ensure the success of your scheme it's worth taking time to analyse what it is that you really need. Think of this as a set of goals you're hoping to achieve – it could be something tangible, such as converting the spare room into a home office, or perhaps it's looser and more emotionally driven, like creating a calm, welcoming space.

Look at the reality of the situation, and be honest with yourself, pinpointing the specific factors that are preventing your current space from meeting these goals. Finances aside (for now), what is actively stopping you from converting the spare room (is it full of furniture you need to clear first?), or from achieving that zen vibe (maybe your current colours or layout are stopping you from feeling relaxed)?

Next, consider what practical aspects are holding you back: maybe you'd like the home office to act as an occasional guest room, but you're not sure how to fit in a sofa bed; or your space doesn't get much natural light, but you can't alter its fundamental layout to alleviate this. Jot everything down, then consider what steps you could take to move forward. In the case of the gloomy space, could shifting focus and making it deliberately dark and cosy solve the low light levels problem? Would a futon in a box be a better compromise for the occasional sleeping requirements in your study?

One of the most important aspects of design – and one that is sometimes overlooked or underestimated – is how our homes can support us on an emotional level. Keep this in mind to focus your ideas and act as an anchor to stop you going off track. For example, if you've decided you want to create a scheme that feels relaxing, but your head is being turned by lots of bright, vibrant tones, drill a little deeper into what you really want, or consider how you could incorporate both in a way that still fulfils those emotional needs.

Doing a design audit as part of your first steps should result in a far clearer and considered idea of what you need.

tip

Physically writing down your thoughts can help your brain process things more clearly. You could even turn it into a journaling exercise, to get the juices flowing.

what's your signature style?

Before getting bogged down with trends and looks, it's worth taking the time to consider what elements make up your personal 'signature style'. It can be helpful to think of this almost like your design DNA. Signature style runs deeper than simply combining a couple of different trends, and is more a representation of who you are and how this is reflected in your aesthetic choices.

Defining your signature style can be an incredibly useful way of taking the stress out of decorating decisions, and even help you get to know yourself a little better. Rather than viewing it as something that limits you to a set look or colour scheme, think of it more as a personal toolkit or reference book to refer back to in moments of uncertainty. Representing both the bigger design picture and the smallest details, it's also important to see your style as something that will evolve as your tastes change and your confidence grows, rather than it being set in stone.

It can take a bit of work to figure this out, as it requires more in-depth analysis than the simplistic magazine quizzes designed to determine whether you're a 'boho' or 'Scandi' type, but you will likely discover that there are certain design styles and colour palettes you're naturally drawn to more than others. Here are some things to consider to help you define yours and build a picture of your broader tastes:

- Are there particular trends, design periods or colours you're drawn to, and can you pinpoint what it is about them that piques your interest? Is it the use of space, or certain tones?
- What are your happy interiors memories, and how might they dictate your design preferences? Do you love retro style because it reminds you of your grandparents' house? Or are you drawn to ditsy florals as you had a favourite flowery comfort blanket as a child?
- Consider your emotional requirements and personality type: if you're very outgoing and love to play host, you

tip

If you're still feeling stuck, ask a few friends or family members how they'd describe your style, then consider whether any common themes are emerging.

may require different design choices to someone who values a calm, cosy corner.

- Picture your ideal vacation: where are you? What are you doing? What sights, sounds and smells are around you, and how are they making you feel? See if any of these elements hold design clues which could relate to your signature style.
- Look inside your wardrobe: what styles and colours of clothing do you go for? Do you like to add lots of bold, colourful accessories, or stick to a simpler look?
- When it comes to cooking, are you experimental, always playing with new flavours and spices, or do you prefer to take comfort in familiar dishes?

It's also worth bearing in mind the signature styles of the other members of your household: unless you live alone, you'll likely need to accommodate the preferences of partners, family members or housemates. While cohabiting with those who have wildly different tastes to yours can be challenging, it's important to find something that works for everyone without inadvertently diluting a potentially stronger scheme or ignoring anyone's tastes. Delve deeper and see if people can identify an emotional connection to their preferred looks (or uncover whether there's an underlying reason they dislike a certain colour or style). From there, see if you can find any common ground, then look at practical ways you might be able to incorporate this so that everyone (at least partially) gets what they want.

'It's important to bring all your design elements together – that's the language that they share.'

Laurence Llewelyn-Bowen, Interior Designer and Guest Judge

Learn more about creating successful colour palettes on pages 68–69.

creating a visual framework

To help you define your signature style, a useful next step is to collate some visuals and turn them into a 'vision board', or a 'concept board'. These can be broadly thought of in two different ways, and, depending on how attuned to your signature style you're feeling, one might work better than the other. If you think you need to focus further to find your signature style, it's worth beginning with a vision board before moving on to a concept board; if you're already fairly clear on this, go straight in with the latter.

Vision board

Vision boards are a universal tool designed to help you tune in to your needs and gain clarity of thought, which in turn helps you determine what you require from your space. Even though the goal here is to create a useful interior design tool, keep your reference images broad, adding photos, artwork, phrases, ephemera or even pressed flowers – anything that calls to you and you feel a resonance with.

The idea is to help you intuitively tap into the emotions behind what you're drawn to, then interpret them once you've finished. For example, if you've incorporated a printout of a calming seascape, consider what drew you to it: did you feel soothed by the gentle blues in its palette, or did it make you crave a feeling of open space?

Concept board

Concept boards are the place to focus a little more on the design requirements of spaces you're planning to decorate, to bring clarity to the overall vibe before you commit to choosing colours and pieces to fill them with.

You might still want to include a non-interiors inspirational image or two, but this is the place to let your imagination run wild and pick out rooms, looks and pieces you love the style of – even if they're completely outside your budget or are a totally different type of property to yours. The idea is to develop a style direction and ensure you're bringing the mood and ideas into your final interior designs without losing any of the creative magic.

tip

Thick card or foam board offers a sturdy surface for vision and concept boards, but equally a sketchbook will do (this is just for you, after all).

'When I'm creating a scheme, I start by collecting inspirational images, but with my "champagne tastes" in mind, so I'll include items that might be way outside of my budget. Then I place everything together to help me see the overall look and make sure I'm happy. Next, I'll start browsing the web for similar pieces which might work (or that I could customise or make) to help me get the look with my "lemonade budget". So, indulge in visuals for your champagne taste but once you know what you're looking for, and what alternative you're prepared to accept, then work out how you can pare it back for your lemonade budget.'

Rochelle Dalphinis, Design Contestant, Series 3

An introduction to interiors

SIOBHAN'S SIGNATURE STYLE

While some of us favour a 'magpie aesthetic' – where there are some broader unifying elements of style or colour, yet the overall look is fluid – others hone a more laser-sharp vision that is instantly recognisable as theirs. Neither is necessarily better, but it can be interesting to look at the portfolio of those who have a noticeably distinctive style and observe all the ways in which this remains consistent across their decorating endeavours.

The space

Series 2 design contestant Siobhan definitely falls into the latter camp, with an immediately identifiable aesthetic – showcased here in the living space of the holiday home she designed in episode 8. A modern building set in a desirable destination, her brief was to create a family-friendly space, which she chose to do in her own signature style: playful, fun and bold for kids yet also glam for the grown-ups.

Get the look

+   Create a statement ceiling that's easy to hang multiple light fittings from. Here, 47x97mm (4x2 in) timber joists were fixed to the existing ceiling, then a wallpapered sheet of MDF was attached to the top with a decorative trim at the edges. The lighting cables were fed through pre-drilled holes, then cup hooks were used to support the individual light flexes from the main 'spider' ceiling pendants. While the style is undoubtedly eclectic, by keeping the shades to two shapes and three colours, it isn't overwhelming.

+   Use embossed picture frame mouldings to create frames around oversized wallpaper pieces or wall mural panels, so they look like huge art installations. This can be a cost-effective way to use designs that might be too expensive to cover your whole walls with.

+   Be consistent with your colour accents: in this space, a warm, green-toned mustard is used across the sofas, curtains and cushions, but also picked up in smaller details, such as elements on the wall murals and design details in the coffee table. Despite its maximalist result, this palette is actually quite restrained, with dark peacock blue acting as the only other dominant colour, while black and white elements bring breathing space to the scheme.

'This is full-on Siobhan. There's something so magical about her work, it makes you want to be your best, most colourful self ... It's joyful because it's so unapologetic.'

Michelle Ogundehin

'What this shows me is that Siobhan understands that if you're doing this deep, dark, saturated look, you've got to go full attack.'

Sophie Robinson, Interior Designer, Colour Expert and Guest Judge

'It's ripping up the rulebook and thinking high-impact drama and glamour ... it's definitely uplifting.'

Matthew Williamson, Interior Designer and Guest Judge

2

Formulating a plan

'Beware copycat interiors when you're identifying your own style, otherwise you'll end up with something that isn't authentic to you. A useful tip is to take an interiors image and break down what the elements you do and don't like are, to help determine your personal preferences.'

Sophie Robinson, Interior Designer, Colour Expert and Guest Judge

Build your brief

Now that you have a clearer idea of your signature style, it's time to move things forward to create a practical plan. When designing for your own home, it can be helpful to take a step back and imagine you're a professional interior designer – but your client is you. This tactic not only minimises emotional dramas, but also helps ensure you stay on track with your own brief.

At the start of any commercial design project – even if it's for a residential space – it's the job of the designer to meet with their client to get a handle on what they want and need, then determine the best way forward. This is to ensure they're not only answering the brief, but are also taking it up a level and pushing the client slightly out of their comfort zone. By identifying and tapping into elements their client didn't even know they needed, the designer can create a final scheme that takes the client's initial thoughts and elevates them.

It is also the designer's job to read between the lines of what their client says, to ensure they're both on the same page: for example, if they say they prefer a minimal design scheme, do they mean that they simply don't like bright patterns, or that they want to ensure there's lots of storage so floors and surfaces aren't cluttered? Equally, watch out for ingrained prejudices or broad generalisations: a client may say they don't like green, whereas there's most likely a shade of green (or indeed any colour) to suit everyone, and it's more about finding the

right tone or quantity, and being mindful of how it's used and what it's paired with.

By placing yourself in the headspace of both designer and client, it can help aid open-minded curiosity and challenge any of your preconceived notions in order to create a space that pushes your creativity forwards.

Dealing with deviations

As the saying goes, the best laid plans often go awry, so it's important to have confidence in your convictions and be able to think on your feet if things turn pear-shaped – whether it's a mishap with builders or just that something hasn't quite turned out how you envisaged.

If an idea isn't working, or something has been measured incorrectly and doesn't fit the space (or looks odd), try to avoid the trap of slavishly ploughing on and pretending the problem doesn't exist, and instead think outside the box to determine how you could turn things around. Again, be objective, as though you were a hired interior designer – would you stick to your tunnel vision, even if in your gut you knew it wasn't working? Or would you take the executive decision to cut your losses and try to come up with a workaround? Changes will eat up both your time and potentially your budget, so bear in mind that indecision can cost on both fronts. There's a courage and confidence in knowing where to draw the line and move on.

'For me, great interior design starts with a forensic psychological examination of: what are the people using this space going to be doing? Why are they here? Who are they with? It's always all about the user.'

Michelle Ogundehin

'Be realistic and honest with yourself and your budget: shop around for trades and negotiate - don't pay their fees all upfront, do it in stages. Once you've got everything in place, stick to the plan as much as you can, though if unforeseen things happen, or you do deviate from the action plan, just be prepared as this is when the budget tends to go walkabout.'

Ry Elliott, Design Contestant, Series 4

Learn more about decorating for mood on pages 170–171.

making a mood board

It's useful to differentiate the inspirational, scene-setting and design direction-defining vision and concept boards (see pages 16–17) from the more practical and detailed mood board – usually made up of both physical samples and images directly related to the look you're planning. Think of your previous boards as a trip to the shop for ingredients, and the mood board as combining it into a meal.

This is where you can get up close and personal with the details and bring all your ideas and samples into one space to see how everything holds together visually. And while it's useful to stick down images, consider a less permanent solution when it comes to physical samples such as wallpapers, fabrics, flooring and paint chips. A tray works brilliantly for this (the designer Kelly Wearstler refers to this as a 'vibe tray', as it contains the essence of the final space).

This fluid approach gives you the flexibility to make changes along the way and handle any samples so you can get a sense of their tactility. View it as an opportunity to play with putting different pieces together to see how they work collectively and how they react to different light; and, by keeping things loose, you can easily take relevant samples along when you're sourcing furniture or accessories.

Based on Nicki's mood board, created for her showhome bedroom design in Series 1, episode 1

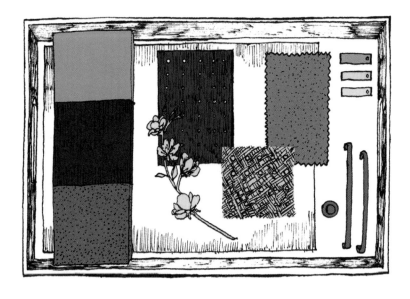

behind the scenes : how to create your own design pack

By Edward Robinson, Design Producer, Interior Design Masters

Part of my job is to visit each space our designers will be working on to pull together a 'design pack' for them, which forms the basis of their schemes. However, this is a useful process to follow for designing your own home, too, and provides you with a suite of handy information for when you need to work out paint quantities and wallpaper requirements or hire a specific tradesperson. Here are the steps we take:

+   Create a comprehensive list of measurements detailing every aspect of the room. As well as the floor plan and wall heights, jot down the dimensions of architectural elements like skirting boards, doors and windows, and fittings such as light switches and plug sockets.

+   Note down measurements of any existing furniture you plan to keep in the space, and ensure you also record measurements of your front door and access routes if you plan on purchasing any large pieces.

+   If you don't feel you're good at visualising how things will work in real life, measure potential furniture and mark its planned placement on your floors with masking tape to help gauge whether it will work in the space.

+   Take photos and videos of everything in its current state: aim for a mixture of wide, full-room shots as well as details of furniture you're retaining, architectural details and fittings (for reference, but it's also always nice to have 'before' shots to look back on!).

+   Make a list of any dos and don'ts for the space, for example an aspect that must be addressed, such as replacing a rotten window frame, alongside anything that can't be touched, like a main incoming electrical supply cable.

+   Use your measurements to create a bird's-eye floor plan, be it a simple sketch or something created in CAD (Computer Aided Design software). Whatever method you use, keep it to scale so you can play with different furniture options and configurations. Keep all this information with your design research, and easily accessible to you and any trades-people you're working with, so everyone is on the same page.

collating research online

While physically collated samples are an invaluable part of the process, and hand-drawn guides (whether a simple graph-paper drawing or an illustrated design scheme) have both validity and charm, there is much that technology can help us with, too.

Perfect pinning

In terms of a space to collate thoughts and ideas, Pinterest is hard to beat for its usability and intuitive algorithm (once it gets a sense of your tastes, it'll feed you a steady stream of similar inspirational ideas). Set yourself up with different folders organised by room or project, and make use of its 'sections' facility, which effectively allows you to round up all the different elements (like furniture, accessories and art) that you might incorporate into the scheme within each board.

Get smart with socials

Instagram can be an equally powerful tool for seeking out and storing interiors ideas. Similar to Pinterest, you can choose to save posts into your own curated folders to build up an archive of themes and ideas. Searching specific hashtags can also be a great way to find inspiration (check out some of the hashtags under the posts of influencers you like to spark new ideas).

TikTok is a brilliant place to seek out quick DIY tutorials and organisation tips from its ever-growing interiors community, with most videos under a minute long – a great option for the time-poor or for those who prefer to watch rather than read.

'If you go to Pinterest as your first port of call and start pinning everything that catches your eye without really knowing what you want, you'll likely end up feeling overwhelmed and stuck. It's much better to go in there with a focused idea, once you've done your homework. I refer to this as "pinning with purpose", and it's a technique I teach to my online students.'

Ju De Paula, Design Contestant, Series 1

tip

Many large retailers are now creating apps using augmented reality and online design tools to help you envisage how their products will look in your space; see what tools the brands you're looking to buy from have to offer.

useful layout tools

Create in Canva

This graphic design platform can help you compile multiple images into a single page and lay them out, so you get a rough idea of how everything holds together. It can be especially useful for looking at potential product purchases together; upload 'cut-out' images (single product shots on a white background) of key furniture and accessories, then adjust everything roughly to scale on the page to give a clear visual reference.

Opt for Adobe

From free, entry-level software like Adobe Express, which works in a similar way to Canva, to the more bells-and-whistles premium professional software like Photoshop and Illustrator, if you're looking to create a more polished presentation of your ideas (for your own benefit or to help any tradespeople envisage the design), Adobe programs are worth exploring.

Style it through SketchUp

This software is the tool of choice for many professional designers, allowing you to create both 2D and 3D illustrated mock-ups of scale room designs (with both free and premium paid options available). A versatile tool, it's used for anything from simple spatial designs to full-blown architect-level renders.

'I use various software packages to help present and communicate my ideas, plan spaces and draw detailed designs and elevations, including Adobe InDesign, Photoshop and Illustrator. I also prepare hard sample boards, as people need to see and touch the finishes they will end up living with. I use SketchUp to create floor plans and 3D models.'

Nicki Bamford-Bowes, Design Contestant, Series 1

'I prefer Photoshop to visually pull together my schemes, but it works just as well to create a physical collage from magazine cuttings and printouts of online images. You could even copy and paste a few photos into Microsoft Word, so you can see everything on one page, if you're not confident in creating a mood board online – you certainly don't need to be fully CAD proficient.'

Rochelle Dalphinis, Design Contestant, Series 3

Planning your project

look at the bigger picture

Even if you're only planning on renovating one room, you should look at your home as a whole and consider the impact of this redesign; will it have any knock-on repercussions for the rest of your space if you're changing the functionality of a room? For example, if you're turning a storage room into a child's bedroom, do you need to make accommodations for all the displaced items elsewhere? Try to factor this in.

It's also useful to keep any longer-term plans in mind: are there areas of your overall home layout right now that really don't work? Even if you're not planning to redecorate anywhere else for a few years, or you don't have the budget to switch rooms round and make structural changes, it's good to keep a longer-term vision in mind in case things do change. And if you do have plans you want to implement a few years down the line, keep these in mind before you go gung-ho into your current room renovations. If you ultimately want to knock down the wall between your dining room and kitchen, for example, it wouldn't make sense to invest in expensive fitted storage across the whole dividing wall just now, and opting for inexpensive freestanding units – which you could relocate in the future should you do the work – might be a wiser move.

As always, keep checking in with yourself and if anything feels like it's ultimately not going to work (either aesthetically or practically), be honest and consider making amends in the early stages (it'll make life far easier in the long run).

'The vibe needs to start the second you walk through the door.'

Sarah Willingham, Entrepreneur, Hospitality Expert and Guest Judge

'Remember to immerse yourself in the space and think about it from all perspectives.'

Michelle Ogundehin

If you're not in a position to make structural changes to your space but want to change the layout, read pages 58–59 for tips on zoning.

what are your restrictions?

It's just as important to be aware of what you can't do, as much as what you'd like to do; viewing this as an objective problem-solving exercise can help prevent you getting tangled in the emotions that often go with having to make compromises.

As well as any personal restrictions – such as budget, time and skill level – some larger home improvement jobs may also require the expertise of qualified professionals, so if you're considering any meatier projects it's worth brushing up on some basic regulations to be aware of.

complying with regulations

+ Building regulations: some jobs require a Building Control Officer to check and approve both construction and technical aspects of building work, to ensure they meet health and safety requirements. They're usually required to oversee extensions of any size, but will sometimes also want to sign-off works such as replacing windows, doors and roof coverings, or electrical changes like fuse box replacements or additional radiators.

+ Permitted development: certain renovations or extension work will fall under 'national permitted development rights', such as extensions within a certain size. These rules are under regular review, so always check with your local council.

+ Planning permission: if proposed work falls outside of permitted development, you'll need to seek planning permission, which determines whether your plans comply with local and national building policies.

+ Technical drawings: you may need to submit Planning and Building Regulation Drawings to aid a planning permission request. The purpose of a Planning Drawing is to visually explain the project to your local planning department, whereas a Building Regulation Drawing goes into more technical detail, such as construction methods, which builders will need to work from to ensure you're keeping compliant. You'll likely need a Chartered Architect, Chartered Surveyor or Structural Engineer to draw these up.

creating a project management spreadsheet

It's often planning and management that ensure the success of an interiors makeover project, just as much as design flair. Taking some of the practical findings from your design pack, now's the time to incorporate them into a full project management spreadsheet to detail all the pertinent information both you and any tradespeople will need to keep your project running smoothly, on schedule and on budget.

Setting up a system

Technology has made it far easier to keep on top of budgets and plans, and the instant totting up of the figures makes it quicker to manage finances than using pen and paper. Here are some tips to get the most from your spreadsheet set-up:

- Microsoft Excel is a great place to start, but if you're working collaboratively, Google Sheets makes it easier to share real-time updates (there is also project management software created with interior designers in mind, but this is aimed more at the professional market).
- For larger projects, create different sheets within the same document for building materials, fixtures and fittings, and planned furniture and accessories purchases, to keep things organised.
- Include columns for delivery lead times and estimated arrival dates.
- Add thumbnail images to the relevant columns of planned furniture and accessories so everyone can see at a glance what's what (you might want to incorporate images of existing pieces you plan to use, too).

Balancing the books

Unless you are lucky enough that money is no object, chances are you'll need to keep your finances in check, even if you're not on a super-stringent budget. Make sure you factor in:

- Delivery costs: building materials especially can be costly to transport and deliver, so check as you go.
- Are there any 'hidden' costs? Will you need to hire a skip or pay for waste removal? Do you need to provide parking permits for builders (which can quickly add up on lengthy jobs)?
- You might find it helpful to break costs down into 'estimate' and 'final' columns, keeping the latter for fixed purchases. This will make it easier to keep track of what's already been spent or is non-negotiable, vs items you could potentially ditch or economise on.

Environmental considerations

Consider the environmental impact of your choices, in terms of both homeware and finishes as well as building materials

used. Could you opt for more sustainable plywood over MDF, or choose a flooring underlay made from recycled fibres? Look at any major household electrical appliances you need, too: while there's an argument for running these until they can no longer be repaired to avoid buying new, older appliances can be less energy efficient and cost more to operate than modern, 'smart' appliances. This can all have a bearing on budget, so factor it in early on.

'I actually enjoy working with a low budget, because it makes me think outside the box. If I had a massive budget I wouldn't be as creative, so I think the restriction plays to my strengths because I can take something that's nothing special and make it look really beautiful.'

Paul Moneypenny, Design Contestant, Series 2

work out a running order

An integral part of your project management document is to determine the order of works required for everything. While it's good planning to include this within your overall document, you might also want to write up a physical checklist – detailing who is responsible for doing what and in which order – and tack it on the wall of the room you're working on. This can be especially useful if there are multiple people working on the project, as you can cross things off as you go.

Generally speaking, jobs are usually divided into 'first fix' (foundational work) and 'second fix' (decorative work) – and yes, you guessed it, the first-fix jobs need to happen at the start. These could include:

First fix
- Building or replacing walls, floors and ceilings
- Laying cables and pipes ready for connecting
- Plastering walls and applying 'mist coats' (an initial watered-down coat of paint which seals the plaster)

Second fix
- Adding finishing wood trims such as skirting boards and wall panelling
- Connecting cables and pipes to their respective face plates and light fixtures, or baths and taps
- Painting walls, floors, ceilings and woodwork; fitting tiles, floor cladding and wallpapers

If your project is purely decorative, you may not need to undertake any first-fix jobs, but if you do, take the opportunity to work out at this early stage where you plan to place furniture, lights and even accessories – if you'd like to add a console into a corner and want it to be illuminated, plan in a well-positioned socket for it now. Equally, if you plan on switching your standard radiator for a vertical design, you'll need to choose the model early on so your pipework can be adjusted before you start your second-fix jobs.

tip

Always check back in on your brief to make sure you're hitting those objectives and haven't gone off-piste, or added in something that is speaking a different design language.

DIY vs GSI

While some aspects of renovations must be undertaken by qualified experts or tradespeople in order to meet health and safety requirements, there's a swathe of tasks that fall into a somewhat grey area. If it's something you technically could do, it's worth weighing up the pros and cons of going for DIY vs GSI ('getting someone in'). You might want to consider:

Time: if you're short of it, is your time more valuable than your money? This is especially relevant if you're self-employed and having to turn down work in order to fit in a gruelling floor-sanding schedule.

Capability: while everyone starts out an amateur and there's a huge satisfaction in learning, it's wise not to go straight in at the deep end. If you've never touched a drill or saw before in your life, maybe avoid making a bespoke fitted storage unit as your first ever project. Consider your physical capabilities, too: if the project will involve lots of heavy lifting, or require several people, is it something you can feasibly manage?

Tools: while there are certain toolkit basics that are well worth investing in (see pages 38–39), if you're looking at undertaking jobs that require expensive or bulky equipment that you might only use once or twice (or have nowhere to store), consider outsourcing the job (or hiring the kit).

Temperament: many of us (readers of this book hopefully included) can feel immense satisfaction in teaching ourselves new skills and trying something different, whether it's painting a mural or upholstering a chair found in a skip. But if you hate certain aspects – like fixing up shelves or stripping woodwork – and you're simply never going to enjoy it, try to outsource them (funds/willing partner permitting).

'Always try DIY'ing to begin with – remember, if you mess it up you can always get someone in then! But be aware of where the line is between specialist skills, such as carpentry, vs something simpler like constructing or customising some flat pack furniture. They are called craftspeople for a reason!'

Temi Johnson, Design Contestant, Series 4

For a lowdown on paint, see pages 106–107.

breaking it down

Still not sure what to tackle and what to hand over? Mull over the following:

Sanding

+ **DIY:** if it's a self-contained project with good ventilation, or you can work one room at a time.

+ **GSI:** if you're sanding floorboards and woodwork throughout an entire house, it'll be much more efficient if you can get this done in one go - ideally with a few people tackling different areas at once to bring down the project timeframe.

Repairing walls

+ **DIY:** if walls have minor holes and imperfections, this can be easily remedied with some filler and sandpaper (or if you're going to be adding decorative finishes like wood panelling, this will hide them anyway).

+ **GSI:** if they're old and crumbly and ultimately need replastering, get a professional to assess.

Electrics

+ **DIY:** minor repairs and 'like-for-like' changes, such as replacing existing light fixtures or light switches (excluding kitchens and bathrooms).

+ **GSI:** any new electrical work must be undertaken by a qualified electrician in order to meet building regulations, while certain alterations will need to be either undertaken or certified by a professional (if in doubt when it comes to electrics or plumbing, always GSI).

Woodwork

+ **DIY:** installing your own shelves, creating an upcycled wooden tabletop or even cladding walls with wood panelling can all be relatively novice-friendly if you follow expert advice (more on all this later).

+ **GSI:** unless you're pretty competent (or keen to learn and willing to invest a chunk of time into the process), it's best to leave bigger projects - such as building storage units with drawers, or creating complex fitted furniture in awkward alcoves - to the pros.

'If I'm calculating how much wood I need for a project, I use a phone app such as SketchCut Pro - you add in the dimensions of the various pieces of wood you need to create your project, then it calculates how to optimise the cuts from standard 120 x 240cm (8 x 4 ft) sheet material.'

Wayne Perrey, Carpenter at The TV Carpenter and Interior Design Masters

Fixed elements

light and views

Natural light makes a huge difference to the way we live in – and feel about – our space. Whether you're planning an extension or undertaking work that will enable you to alter how light enters your home, it's important to give this aspect careful consideration. And if you're simply trying to make the most of what you've got, there are lots of ways to harness this, too.

Pay close attention to the way the daylight hits your interiors, from the easterly corners that pick up the cool yet intense morning sun to the spots that get bathed in a golden glow when it sets in the west. South-facing rooms will likely enjoy bright but regularly changing light and shadows throughout the day, while north-facing rooms offer a more even, consistent and distilled light.

If you've got spaces that are particularly gloomy (and you can't extend), see if you can borrow natural light from elsewhere: could you replace solid internal doors with glass (or a transom window above), or partially knock through two reception rooms and fit glazed doors across the opening? Ensure what light you do have isn't obscured by furniture or window treatments covering glazing even when open. Depending on your space, could you add a roof light or 'sun tunnel', which

A cosy window corner in the living room designed by Barbara in Series 2, episode 1

borrows light from other areas? If none of these is an option, try the cosy route instead, bringing in rich jewel tones and lots of textiles to embrace its darker looks. If it's possible, consider switching room uses – a dim bedroom, where you mainly spend your time asleep anyway, might be more palatable than a dark family room.

'For a space you only really use in the evenings, or for a cosy room like a snug or TV den, I'd go fully wraparound with a black or dark colour across both walls and ceiling for an immersive feel.'

Dean Powell, Design Contestant, Series 3

Formulating a plan

planning for fitted storage

Whatever your needs and style preference, decent storage is a crucial element of any interiors scheme, and is best factored into the early planning stages rather than leaving as an afterthought.

Take this opportunity to plan in as much fitted storage as you can, ideally incorporating a range of options, from (depending on the room) at least one full-height cupboard for mops, upright vacuums, ladders and ironing boards, to sneaky bonus cupboards or ledges carved out of space that might otherwise have just been boxed in. Consider which areas feel like natural spots to incorporate storage, and how it works with the flow of the space. Unless it's something you want to turn into a feature or use for open display, it's best kept as unobtrusive as possible – place cupboards somewhere even slightly tricky to access, or in an awkward spot, and you run the risk of living with perpetual clutter and piles of items waiting to be put away.

Also consider your preferred living style and stress threshold: while one person might feel more relaxed in a completely clutter-free space, devoid of visual noise and distractions, for someone else this could feel cold compared to their preferred lived-in look, surrounded by the many things they love which give them great joy. It's important to differentiate, however, between treasured possessions and clutter – and while this might be somewhat open to interpretation, there's generally never an aesthetic reason to have your dirty laundry, piles of mail or cleaning supplies out on show full-time. Consider too the placement of furniture; to help aid a feeling of space and flow, try to avoid the sides of furniture being the first thing you see when you walk into the room, which can be visually jarring. If layout means there's really no choice, try disguising the visible side by painting or wallpapering it to match your walls.

Planning built-in storage from the start is particularly wise for tricky areas such as loft conversions, and other spaces with eaves creating below head-height corners, or rooms with unusual footprints which would make buying perfectly fitting

tip

If you want to add hidden storage inside a shallow alcove, but there's not enough functional space to incorporate a door front (or you're not able to make those sort of changes), try hanging a floor-to-ceiling curtain across its front instead, secured on a tension rod.

fake something fitted

If you're on a tight budget and want to create the look of bespoke fitted furniture but haven't the time or skills to make it from scratch, see if you can fake it by combining shop-bought pieces with wooden trims and moulding strips to create a built-in look. Search online for 'IKEA hacks' for a plethora of ideas that use basic bookcases and cupboards to create personal looks, which can easily be applied to other furniture brands.

Ju styled this freestanding wardrobe to look fitted in by boxing in the top to make it flush to the ceiling in her student bedroom redesign, in Series 1, episode 4

freestanding pieces difficult. For small spaces in particular, going with floor-to-ceiling storage can help the overall space feel calmer and reduce the risk of clutter being shoved on furniture tops and letting down the overall look. For large areas of storage or entire storage walls, consider a best-of-both-worlds approach with a mixture of open sections for displaying favourite items and objet, and closed

storage for the pieces you'd rather keep tucked away.

'When you're designing tight, small spaces, every little inch counts – buying furniture from the shops can be quite a waste of space if it doesn't maximise the storage.'

Jerome Gardener, Design Contestant, Series 1

Toolkit essentials

know your kit

Whether you've just moved into your first home or have accrued a few hammers and screwdrivers along the way but need to level up your kit, it can be confusing knowing what's worth investing in.

Your budget and the work you're planning to do will play a big part in what to buy, but if you're in a small space (or have limited funds) it can also be prohibitive to own too many tools, especially bulkier items. Think creatively: could you kit-share 'occasional' items like a tall ladder or floor sander with a few friendly neighbours? If you are looking to make some purchases, here are some items to consider:

Perfect prep

Floor and furniture protection: old bedsheets and flattened cardboard boxes laid on the floor are perfectly adequate, though plastic sheets can help protect soft furnishings against paint spills. Corrugated floor protection sheets are worth sourcing if heavy-duty building work is going on.
PPE: goggles and face masks are a must when working with chemicals or if you're creating lots of dust (especially around carcinogenic materials like MDF). You may also need to wear protective gloves if working with any potentially toxic liquids.

Stripping paint: sandpaper should suffice for smaller jobs (the lower the grit, the coarser it is, so stick to lower numbers for heavy sanding and higher numbers for finishing surfaces). An electric hand-held mouse sander is useful for fixtures and furnishings with moulded edges. Bigger jobs would benefit from an electric heat gun to strip paint, or a chemical paint stripper for more intricate surfaces like fireplaces.

Tools

Hammer: a magnetic claw hammer is a good all-rounder, but if you're working on bigger jobs like installing flooring, a nail gun could be a wise investment.
Screwdrivers: a mixed set with different sizes of flat head, Phillips and Pozidriv will cover all bases, while a ratchet multi-bit screwdriver is a great toolkit all-rounder, especially for repetitive work.
Glue: glue guns are inexpensive and work well for a range of DIY uses, from bonding woods and fabrics together to sticking down flooring, as well as in multiple craft projects (where you can also use coloured or glitter glue sticks, if that's your vibe). PVA is a great all-round adhesive that can also be mixed with sawdust and used as a filler, as well as applied as surface protection

tips from the trade: which drill?

By Wayne Perrey, Carpenter at The TV Carpenter and Interior Design Masters

If you're planning any DIY, I'd advise investing in a good combination drill in the £70-100 price bracket. These models have three functions: hammer (allowing you to drill through brickwork), drill (for creating holes in wood) and screwdriver (for tasks like fitting flat-pack furniture together). Always get battery-operated over mains-powered - modern batteries are very powerful and long lasting, but ensure you have a spare so you can charge one while you work with the other. To save money in the long run, stick to the same brand for all your power tool purchases, so they can share battery packs.

when watered down. General wood glue is suitable for most woodworking jobs, while heavy-duty mount glue is a great alternative to nails and screws for various DIY applications that are no-/low-load bearing.

Knives: Stanley knives with retractable blades work well for most cutting applications, though knives with rubber-coated handles and built-in spare blade storage are handy to have.

Saws: the humble hacksaw is an inexpensive basic for most small cutting jobs, while a coping saw is great for detail work, such as cutting out creative design shapes. Bigger jobs will likely require a power saw: a circular saw is a good option where space is limited, as it's versatile and easy to transport, while a mitre saw allows you to make specific cuts at designated angles. A saw track and guide can be a worthwhile investment if you have lots of straight lines to cut.

'Biodegradable baby wipes are invaluable to have on hand when you're decorating or doing DIY for instantly clearing up spills and splashes.'

Fran Lee, Design Contestant, Series 3

Learn how to build your own storage seating on pages 60–61.

3

Layout
and colour

'Interior design is about how a room feels, not simply the colours you paint the walls.'

Michelle Ogundehin

Space set-ups by room

go with the flow

While you might now be itching to dive straight into picking paint colours and choosing cushions, take a moment to consider the bigger picture of both the space you're looking to decorate and how it might work with the overall layout and flow of your home. Fundamental elements you might otherwise not think about can be crucial to the success of any spatial design: it's all very well having a beautiful looking family room, but if you're having to climb over multiple obstacles to access it, or the layout isn't conducive to family interaction, no amount of pleasing decor is going to remedy that.

Designers often talk about having 'good flow' when it comes to home design, but if that's something you find hard to conceptualise, try a practical test and go for a walk around your space as it is now: are you being forced to veer off from natural walkways due to a slightly too-big side table or a perpetual pile of shoes? Are there any abandoned corners you rarely go to and, if so, could you remedy this by adding in some seating or storage? Often we get very used to these minor irritations or under-utilised spots, so try to figure out what yours are along with the other members of your household.

Once you've got a clearer idea of your movements, this can help form the basis of your floor plans and indicate where the best spots might be for different activities. Notice what vistas or details your eye is naturally drawn to within this new flow – is there scope for rethinking the placement of appealing artwork or unsightly storage, depending on what's now in your eyeline? You might find, especially in smaller homes, that there's not much opportunity for making drastic changes, or it might spur you to bite the bullet and switch entire rooms around.

'One of the things interior design has to prove to itself is its practicality.'

Laurence Llewelyn-Bowen, Interior Designer and Guest Judge

make an entrance

As any estate agent will tell you, kerb appeal can have a huge impact on how others view your home; but, more importantly, creating an exterior and entrance area that pleases you – both aesthetically and practically – is an often overlooked step in setting the mood for your whole home. Simply repainting a shabby front door and planting out a few pretty flowerpots can help you feel happier before you're even inside.

While hallways are often limited in space, consider what elements you can include – both to draw the eye through them and minimise any organisational niggles. Some storage is a must, even if it's confined to a slimline radiator cover with a shelf top, or a few hooks for keys and coats. Strategic use of colour on walls can be the best way to set up design moments, so look at how either pattern or simple paint effects can contribute to the overall feel. Designing with a sense of totality, considering the journey through your home, can help everything hold together and tell the story of you; this can be achieved through small details which share a 'red thread', rather than overtly using the same colours or styles in every room.

Space specifics

- Low-level lighting brings even light to a hallway, especially at night-time. Factor this into the first-fix stage of building work and see if you can integrate recessed lighting into stair treads or skirting boards.
- Consider how the colours used in a hallway impact the rooms leading off it: opting for a darker hallway can help other spaces feel lighter and brighter upon entry, or, conversely, keeping your hallway light can help a dark-painted living room feel even cosier as the eyes have to adjust.
- If your front door opens directly into a living area, strategically arrange any solid-backed furniture to the left or right of the door to create a corridor effect and visually zone off the area – as seen in Paul Moneypenny's cafe redesign in Series 2, episode 7 (see illustration, above).

living rooms

Increasingly, our living rooms are multi-use spaces and are required to act as both a social hub and a private sanctuary, possibly with some home hot-desking or toddler-wrangling for good measure.

It's important to create a space that feels safe and comforting (alongside any practical safety needs). While you might not be consciously aware of it, sitting on a sofa with your back to the door – or, conversely, directly facing it – could subconsciously leave you feeling on edge. Instead, try positioning any seating so you're able to see the entrances but are not directly facing towards or away from them. Bear in mind other sightlines, too: if you can see through to adjoining or adjacent rooms, while they needn't necessarily match, be mindful of how each of their individual designs might impact on the other – whether that's via a loosely connected colour palette or elements from similar design styles or periods.

In a living space, many of us tend to point all our furniture towards the TV, at the expense of creating more interesting,

intimate nooks. If you have a beautiful view from a window, or a stunning feature fireplace, consider ways you can re-orient the layout to at least incorporate this, or set up a smaller seating nook away from the main sofa area.

Cosy configurations

In most living rooms, sofas and seating form the most important element (yes, OK, the TV, too!). There's a lot more than appearance to consider if you're shopping for a new suite, however. Bear in mind:

- Consider your preferred seating style when deciding on both the aesthetics and cushioning of your seating: are you a lounger who loves to spread out, or do you tend to curl up, cat-like, in the corner? Do you love a cheeky afternoon sofa nap, or prefer to sit up straight with a supported back and neck?
- Would your whole family enjoy piling onto one super-sized statement sofa, or would a smaller suite with a choice of armchairs and accent chairs work better to

'An easy trap to fall into is to just start shopping – you need to begin with the bigger picture.'

Matthew Williamson, Interior Designer and Guest Judge

give everyone their own space?

- If your room is small, a large-as-you-can corner couch could be a good bet: visually, a larger L-shaped sofa reads as one object, rather than several smaller seating options which could contribute to a cluttered feel.

- Consider the delivery practicalities: if you're in a flat, or have difficult access, a modular suite that can be assembled in-situ might make more sense.

Space specifics

- Focus on whether you'd prefer a space that's set up symmetrically or not: a symmetrical layout is generally more calming on the eye (as it's simpler for us to process), but it also runs the risk of looking a little dull. Symmetrical styles naturally look more formal, so if you're after a traditional or heritage feel – think two identical sofas placed opposite one another – try this route, but if you're creating a relaxed boho vibe it might not work. As a general rule of thumb, if you're going with symmetry, make sure it's bang on, whereas if you're opting for asymmetry it needs to be very deliberately 'off', so be aware of your spacing.

- Watch for proportions of furniture and accessories; ensure everything has a proportional relationship, unless you are purposely looking to add a dramatic or playful feel with something that's super-sized or very small.

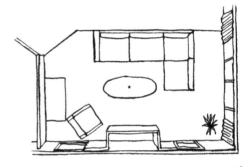

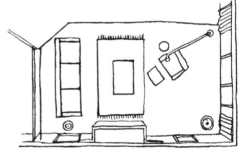

Despite the identical footprints, both design teams went for different living room configurations to best suit the needs of each space, as seen in Series 1, episode 5.

See pages 226–227 for ideas on how to hide your tech.

kitchens and bathrooms

Generally, both kitchen and bathroom renovations tend to fall into two main camps: the full-on redesign, where you'll likely be employing tradespeople to gut the existing space and start again from scratch, or even fit them fresh into a new extension; or the DIY makeover approach (titivating, rather than replacing).

The former comes with the benefit of having professionals on hand to turn to for advice, but of course is far more costly – and arguably a little less creatively challenging – than a makeover. In some instances (and if you have the budget), existing rooms do warrant total replacement, such as if plumbing is leaking behind walls or cabinets are rotten. But before you reach for the sledgehammer it's worth considering whether you really do need to rip it out and start again, or if, for the sake of your pocket and the planet, you can create the space you desire with a more hands-on approach.

What to do with walls?

Humidity and splashes mean kitchen and bathroom walls require specialist surfaces or treatments – though you're not just limited to tiles. Here are a few ideas:

- Wallpaper: yes, you can use wallpaper in kitchens and bathrooms … with a few exemptions. A non-woven paper will fare best, finished with a coat of matt water-

based varnish for extra protection (though it's still best avoided in particularly humid spaces, or anywhere it will come into more than the odd splash of water).

- Splashbacks: more commonly used in kitchens, splashbacks can also work for a fuss-free look in a bathroom. Splashbacks can be easier to install than tiles as they're generally just one solid piece, and they also require less maintenance. They can even offer the chance for a bit of creativity; seek out hand-painted glass or acrylic versions, which can feature decorative paint effects or illustrated designs.

- Specialist plaster: if you love the look of rustic limewashed walls, opting to finish walls with tadelakt – a traditional Moroccan wall surfacing technique – creates a completely waterproof surface finish that's suitable for use above sinks and inside shower cubicles. For a wraparound look, use microcement on floors (it looks similar, but is more durable).

Surface-deep fixes

When it comes to cladding, contact paper is your best friend. A decorative vinyl adhesive-backed paper, it can be adhered to a number of different kitchen and bathroom surfaces, including cupboard door fronts, work surfaces, counter and cabinet tops, and tiles. You can even get creative and cut out your own bespoke designs. Inexpensive and available in a range of colours and styles,

it usually removes without damaging the original surface, too, making it a great option for renters. However, there are a few other relatively simple refreshes to try:

Painted cabinets, replacement handles and tile decals made from contact paper triangles were all used in this student kitchen revamp in Series 1, episode 4

- Change the look of built-in cabinetry with paint: brushing or rolling it on, or opting for spray paint, is arguably the easiest way to do this, though – depending on the cupboard's original make-up (and the paint you use) – you may need to sand and prime it first (see page 106 for details on how best to do this).
- Prefer a paint-free solution? Consider replacing cupboard doors entirely; there's an increasing number of companies offering inexpensive new door fronts in a range of on-trend colours and finishes. Replacing doors-only is less wasteful than ripping out entire kitchen carcasses.
- Replace tired old handles and drawer pulls with something a little smarter for an instant upgrade, or try glitzing up existing handles with a coating of spray paint in a luxe metallic finish or bold hue.
- Use a grout pen for an easy refresh, whether it's to make existing grouting look fresher (far less effort than re-grouting) or to switch up the look of your tiled area with a bold new colour. The latter works well against standard white tiles, to make them appear like a more deliberate choice.

'If you can work with existing fittings, why get rid of them? In the home I designed in episode 7, I left the original kitchen doors alone but customised them with new rustic rope handles to get the look I wanted.' (Shown on page 101.)

Paul Andrews, Design Contestant, Series 3

planning a kitchen

Key considerations

- Layout-wise, keep in mind the 'work triangle': a space where the sink, fridge and cooker are all within a few paces of each other is generally considered the most user-friendly. Unless you're fully renovating you might not be able to do much about your sink and cooker, but if you're missing this triangle in your existing layout, could you maybe move your fridge to get the space working better?

Space specifics

- Wall cabinets can look clunky, and in recent years many homeowners have removed theirs in favour of open shelving for a less formal look. While this undoubtedly creates a more blended feel, consider your storage needs (and what will end up on display) if you make the switch. To try before you buy, think

Old fruit crates used as wall shelves by Paul, Series 2, episode 7

about removing cabinet doors and simply painting the carcasses to see if open shelving works for you.
- For a streamlined look, consider one long mono shelf that wraps across a whole wall rather than several short, stubby ones – though take the work triangle into account (you don't want to be hiking 50 paces from your kitchen tap every time you want to get a glass for water).
- Try DIY-ing your own kitchen island as an alternative solution to a built-in. Screw several old wooden fruit crates together and add castors to the bottom to create a flexible, rustic piece, or place a couple of kitchen base units directly on the floor then add on a fitted wood offcut as a worktop.

planning a bathroom

Key considerations

- As with kitchens, there might be little you can do about an inherited bathroom layout, and, even if you are replacing everything from scratch, it could be prohibitively expensive to move key plumbing or soil pipes. If your set-up isn't ideal, consider smaller switches which could help things to work better: add in freestanding storage cabinets if there's nothing built in, switch out a grotty shower curtain for a sleeker glass screen, or replace a tiddly mirror with a large, glazed cabinet.
- If you're refitting a small bathroom, look for ways to increase the feeling of spaciousness without sacrificing luxury: a petite roll top bath could fit into a smaller gap than you think, while opting for a wall-mounted toilet with concealed cistern will look less cluttered.
- Bathroom lighting needs careful consideration in order to meet safety requirements. Broadly speaking, any lighting within a couple of metres of a bath or shower (known as Zone 1) will require light fittings rated IP65, while beyond this (Zone 2) should be fine with IP44 (but always check before purchasing). Traditionally, IP65/44-rated lighting designs have been limited, but there has been a broad increase in styles in recent years, so this restriction shouldn't mean limiting your look.

Small shower space by Paul, Series 3, episode 5

Space specifics

- No space for a radiator in a tiny bathroom? Try fitting electric underfloor heating mats both under the floor and wall tiles (outside of shower and bath surrounds), to keep things toasty.
- Bathrooms can often feel clinical, so add some softness with cosy hammam towels and plump rug-style bathmats. Accessorising with plants and ornaments helps to soften the look, too.
- While replacing bathroom suites is a big job, switching out taps and shower heads is a lot less hassle (and cost). Both brass and black fittings have become increasingly popular, though the former can be expensive: save funds by shopping around – as long as your fittings all share the same design language, it doesn't matter if they don't match exactly.

dining room

Having a room dedicated solely to dining is increasingly becoming a luxury, and in today's ever-shrinking, busy homes it's as likely to be required for homework and hot-desking as it is dining and socialising. It's important to keep this flexibility in mind and decide on your priorities as well as your willingness (or lack thereof) to reconfigure layouts throughout the day vs opting for fixed-in-place furnishings.

Consider what's going to be in your eyeline whether sitting or standing – a whole wall of artwork or a patterned wallpaper might be more interesting at both levels than a couple of high-up paintings, but if it's also a study space, will a bold pattern be too distracting?

A multi-use raised breakfast bar in the open-plan kitchen/living space designed by Fran Lee and Peter in Series 3, episode 1

design your own dining table

Creating your own table can be a brilliant way to get something that meets your exact size specifications - and it needn't necessarily cost more than buying one off-the-shelf. You can easily source table legs online - around 70cm (27in) is a good height - from individual legs and trestle-style sets to DIY-free options, which attach directly to tabletops with an inbuilt clamping screw.

See if your local timber yard can create a custom top for you, or, for something more rough and ready, turn several shelves or scaffold boards into a long tabletop using battens on the underside to hold them together. You could also get creative and source some architectural salvage, such as an old door, to use as a top. If it has a characterful yet not exactly wipe-clean patina, pop some polished-edge Perspex sheet on top for protection.

Which table type?

TYPE	BEST FOR
Round	Square rooms, to break up the blockiness, and for tables situated in through-rooms, to minimise banging into sharp corners. Ideally avoid anything less than 110cm (43in) diameter, unless you're going for a table-for-two bistro look in a small corner.
Rectangular	Versatility: rectangular tables can be easily tucked against the wall when you want to clear some floorspace, or set up in the centre of your room for social dining. If you want styling space for a table runner, go for a generous 90cm (35in) width.
Square	Smaller households (opt for an extendable square table or double drop leaf table so you're covered for when guests come round).
Oval or pill-shaped	Spaces where you'd like a rectangular-shaped table rather than round or square, but want to avoid walking directly into edges.
Wall-mounted drop leaf	Super-small spaces, or rooms where you'll gain more benefit from the extra floor space than having a permanent table fixed in place (you could consider adding wall hooks next to it to store folding chairs, too).

Space specifics

As tables are generally large and blocky, planning the flow around a dining space is important. To ensure no one feels hemmed in, allow at least 70–80cm (27–31in) between chair backs and walls, and a minimum of 60cm (24in) per place setting.

If you're short on space, banquette seating or benches work well. An L-shaped banquette can also be useful for marking out a dining area within a multi-use room. Sneaking in a breakfast bar against the back of an L-shaped worktop with a couple of bar stools is a great table alternative.

bedrooms

A flat fabric canopy looks chic and modern in this bedroom designed by Amy, Series 3, episode 1

Whatever your style, most people prefer a sleeping space that feels relaxing and minimises any stressors, so anything that could detract from getting a good night's sleep should be avoided. When planning a bedroom, give this aspect just as much consideration as design and aesthetics.

Your bed will undoubtedly be the largest element of your room. Where possible, try placing it with the bedhead against a solid wall rather than a window, with both sides accessible, and ideally not directly opposite the door (which can leave you feeling subconsciously vulnerable). If you're short on space for bedside tables on either side, wall mount some slim shelves instead and opt for wired-in wall lights (go for lower lumen red-toned bulbs, which will help you relax ready for sleep).

To eliminate clutter, try to incorporate as much concealed storage as possible by utilising floor-to-ceiling cupboards as well as any hidden areas like under the bed (though use this space intentionally, not just as a dumping ground). Go a step further and try painting built-in storage the same colour as your walls so it all but disappears, leaving you with a serene space. Alternatively, hide cupboards in plain sight by covering them in wallpaper if they're flat-fronted. If you've already got a bedframe without integrated storage, seek out shallow storage boxes to tuck underneath it, or – if it's an area that's

visible – repurpose some pretty vintage suitcases to store things in instead, which can be easily pulled out for access.

There's often a balancing act between creating a space that feels conducive to relaxation, yet also energises us when required. Your choice of bed dressing can be one way to add in a flash of drama: bring in patterned duvet covers and throws when you feel you need a visual lift, which is then easy to tone down by switching to a simpler throw if it feels a little overwhelming. Consider keeping any very busy patterns or saturated colours contained within accents and accessories only, so you aren't distracted by an unwieldy pattern just as you're trying to doze off.

headboard hacks

Shop-bought headboards can be expensive, but if you're prepared to get stuck into a little DIY you can achieve an impressive look for a lot less money which is the perfect fit for your space, too.

+ Get the feel of a four-poster bed without the potentially cumbersome posts by creating a fabric canopy to frame the bed. Suspend two dowelling poles from your ceiling with strong ceiling hooks, with one pole above your bedhead where it meets the wall and the other at least two thirds of the way down the ceiling. Drape the fabric across it, letting it hang down, and stitch on some curtain heading tape if you want a generously ruched look. To save on sewing, use a ready-hemmed flat sheet instead of off-the-roll fabric.

+ Play with scale: bringing out a headboard across the whole width of your wall feels luxurious and can make the space seem bigger. Mount some upholstery foam onto MDF with spray glue, staple your chosen fabric across it, then fix it to your wall by attaching D-ring picture hooks to its underside, near the top. Ensure you fix screws of the appropriate weight into your wall at the points where the headboard needs to hang, to rest the D-rings on. If you're going big, create it in sections to stop it getting too heavy and unwieldy.

+ After something intricate? Draw your own bespoke outline onto a sheet of thick upholstery foam, then cut it out using an electric bread knife. Cut some MDF to the same size, then fix in place as above (see pages 218-221 for a guide to upholstery).

+ Headboards can also be hard: use wooden panelling to frame your bed area in place of a physical board, then layer up lots of loose cushions in front for comfort.

+ Make sure your headboard is an appropriate size for the space, especially if going for an oversized look: go too small and it can look mean and throw the whole look off.

'I like to put patterned wallpaper behind the bed so you get that "wow" factor when you walk in, but when you're in bed you're looking out onto a space that's quite restful.'

Jerome Gardener, Design Contestant, Series 1

nurseries and children's rooms

Children's rooms can sometimes feel like the ultimate aesthetic challenge, but, while you might want to give them freedom to choose their own styles, especially as they get older, there's no harm in providing a bit of structured guidance and making sure they have the storage solutions to (at least theoretically) keep things tidy.

The needs of a newborn are, of course, very different to those of an independent teen. Here are a few aspects to consider for the rooms of children of all ages:

Nurseries

- Consider design details from the eyeline of a baby or toddler: could you go to town with a patterned ceiling, or add a design accent, such as painted stripes, on the lower thirds of all walls? Treating these with a busier paint colour or pattern can also help minimise grubby handprints.
- Think future-proofing and repurposing as much as possible: decant nappies and wipes from their often-garish packaging into open-topped fabric storage baskets, or temporarily convert an adult's wardrobe into something suitable for baby clothes by adding tension rode inside it for extra hanging space for little outfits. (And always ensure any nursery modifications meet Health and Safety requirements.)
- Don't forget to create an adult-friendly cosy corner for late-night feeds: a comfy rocking chair seat can feel cocooning.

Child's space

- Avoid decorating the space too heavily in any themed characters or motifs they might suddenly take great umbrage against, and keep key colours and design elements relatively neutral to allow for easy layering in (and subsequent removal of) any current favourites.
- If their bedroom needs to double as a play space, introduce interactive elements which won't make too much mess: try painting one wall (or the below-dado section throughout the room) with chalkboard paint, whiteboard surface paint, or magnetic surface paint – then let them experiment!
- Storage is your friend: boxes and bags made from softer materials like felt and rattan look far more appealing than garish plastic (and are more planet-friendly, too). Utilise any and all available nooks and crannies, from cupboard tops to backs of doors. Large, fitted wardrobes can be good future-proof options: if their clothes aren't filling them just yet, use that extra space for storing toys and games.

Teenage den

- If they sleep in a single bed, try placing it lengthways against a wall so they can style it as a day bed when friends come round, lining decorative cushions along the back and placing pillows at either end to look like bolsters. To maximise a small

A contemporary use of pink in a child's room, designed by Jerome, Series 1, episode 1

space opt for a raised bed, or create a platform for it, with space underneath for extra storage.

- Want them to express themselves but not too keen on wall-to-wall peeling posters? Set them up with a cork wall for tacking all their posters and art prints to. Source some self-adhesive cork tiles, which can be stuck directly to walls (try putting some lining paper up first if you're worried about damage to plaster). For added interest, cut them into a geometric shape before sticking down.

- Trundle beds, or futons in a box, can be a great way to add extra sleeping space for overnight guests and give your teen a sense of independence, as they can set this up themselves.

'Kids basically aren't kids – they're mini adults, with loads of opinions.'

Fran Lee, Design Contestant, Series 3

Layout and colour

home office

Whether you've managed to dedicate an entire room to a home-working space/side hustle/burgeoning business empire, or your 'home office' consists of your laptop perched on whatever surface you find vacant, there's plenty you can do to create a study space that's both functional and good looking.

Even if you do have a separate room, you may still need to share it with a remote-working partner, or occasionally give over the space to overnight guests or an online exercise class, so it's worth keeping things flexible. But whether your desk is going into a home office, a corner of your bedroom, or tucked elsewhere in a multi-use space, the same principles apply.

While your basic set-up should be ergonomically sound, that doesn't limit you to office furniture, which is often ugly: home furniture retailers now increasingly stock style-led desks for the home, but a console table, vintage bureau, antique

A bold home office designed by Abi and Dean, Series 3, episode 1

writing desk or even a small rectangular dining table could all do the job. Add on a monitor riser – look online for chic plywood options, or fashion your own from a shelf resting on a couple of wooden battens – and incorporate some equally homely-looking storage on the top (think charming old tins used as pen pots, and box files re-covered in pretty fabric, to lose the stolen-from-the-stationery-cupboard vibe) and you're good to go.

Zone it out

If you're having to incorporate a workspace into another room, see if you can hide things away: could you customise a large cupboard with a computer shelf, so you can literally close the door on it at the end of each day? Bonus points if you can fit your work chair in the bottom too, but if not keep a throw handy for covering it out-of-hours. Alternatively, seek out a room divider to screen the whole lot off

(mentally, adapting your space like this can help you transition from work to home mode, too). If your desk lacks storage, and it matches your aesthetic, fix up a simple table skirt to hide printers and archive paperwork underneath.

A room with a view

If you do have space, consider placing your desk away from walls and corners in favour of boldly situating it in the middle of the room. Sitting in a corner can feel uninspiring and even lonely, so a view out of a window (or towards the door) can feel more dynamic. However, if a tucked-away corner is your only real option, make it more like a cosy sanctuary by adding a colourful, patterned or customisable backdrop to give your eyes something stimulating to look at, and bring in playful accents like succulents and a quirky desk lamp to liven things up.

tip

Struggling to carve out any workspace at all? See if there's somewhere you could fix up an unobtrusive shelf at desk height (just make sure it's deep enough to accommodate your laptop), then borrow a chair from another room when you need to work. Or do without the chair altogether and fix it at standing height to create your own standing desk. You can always dress the shelf with a few books and ornaments when not in use, to help it blend in with the rest of your space.

multi-use and open-plan spaces

Without the structure of walls, it can feel more daunting trying to set up home in a space that is essentially just one big box. Flexible thinking and strategic use of zoning techniques are best deployed here, to help provide structure and to clarify the intended functionality of each area while still retaining the sense of fluidity that makes open-plan living a popular concept in the first place.

Dividers are incredibly useful tools which are often deployed by designers to help break up an expansive space, or to create much-needed extra nooks in more bijou homes. Whether you're up for some extensive DIY or simply want to shop-and-style, here are a few options.

DIY

- Use wooden battens to create a slatted wall, which allows you to see through it yet still visually divides the space. Build a framework for the slats using battens of the same material, which you'll need to attach to your ceiling, wall and floor to ensure it's secure (the best fixings to use will depend on its intended final size and weight). Then cut the slats so they fit inside the framework before screwing into position: to save time, work out your lengths in advance and order them pre-cut from a timber merchant, and prime/paint each individual length before constructing.

Repurposing

- Think outside the box: look in architectural salvage yards for any interesting items you could use to create a visual divide, such as the vintage wooden pub screen design contestant Banjo used in Series 3, episode 2 to zone off a small seating area within a bedroom space.
- Use curtains as a more textural room divider. Sheer fabrics can be a great option if you want to retain some visibility and avoid blocking the light (and they can usually be supported on simple tension wires); for something with more substance, go for a thicker fabric and get creative with its hanging mechanism – fixing a copper pipe across the space, for example, held in place with hanging rail end sockets. If your fabric can be left fixed in place, it needn't necessarily be curtains at all – repurposed tablecloths or flat sheets can work out a lot cheaper than buying fabric by the metre. Fix a slim wooden batten onto your ceiling, then simply staple it into position.

Decor

- While not a physical divide, colour can be cleverly used to demarcate different zones by using different tones across walls and ceilings to trick the eye into reading

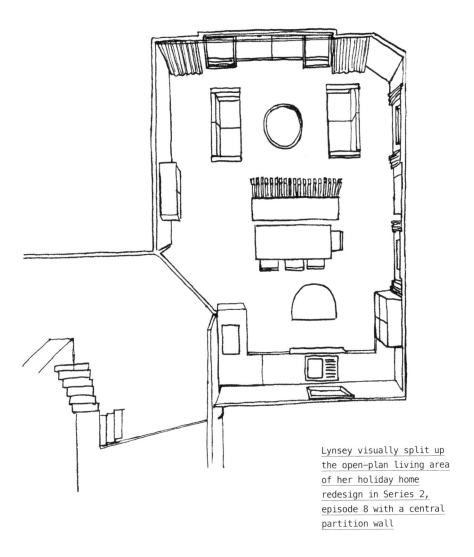

Lynsey visually split up
the open-plan living area
of her holiday home
redesign in Series 2,
episode 8 with a central
partition wall

the space as separate sections. This can be done in a playful way to blur the set boundaries of the space, such as bringing triangular bands of colour across walls and ceilings or using punchy stripes.

- Rugs work wonderfully to define lounging and dining spaces. To maximise their effectiveness go as big as you can so all the furniture within that zone sits on them, rather than inadvertently creating

a sad looking 'carpet island'.

- Bookshelves set up so their short side is against the wall and the shelves protrude into the space can make great room dividers. Place two identical bookcases back-to-back (or decorate the room-facing back of a single bookcase with paint or wallpaper so it feels like a partition wall), or alternatively opt for an open-backed cube bookcase design.

box clever with cube seating

Furniture with multiple uses can be a helpful ally in any space, especially those that are small or open plan. Bespoke cube seating offers a flexible solution to both seating and storage, and once you understand the basic principles of how they are made (see below), you can create a custom design that optimises your own needs.

tips from the trade: how to create your own box

By Wayne Perrey, Carpenter at The TV Carpenter and Interior Design Masters

You will need:

+ Timber or OSB (Oriented Strand Board): choose sturdy processed sheet wood such as birch ply, MDF or OSB. Generally it's best to work with wood that's 18mm (0.7 in) thick

+ Circular electric saw with a track guide rail (or order the specific lengths you need pre-cut)

+ Electric drill and countersunk drill bits

+ Wood glue and wood screws (a 4mm/0.16in wide stainless steel countersunk screw approx. 50mm/2in length should do)

+ Upholstery foam, wadding and fabric for fitted seat pads, if using

+ Castors, if you're creating a moveable seat (I recommend ball bearing castors with 360 swivel rotation)

+ Tape measure, steel ruler, pencil

Method

1. Work out the length, height and depth you want your cube to be. Your side panels will be sandwiched between the top and bottom panels, so for a true square you'll need to deduct the thickness of the top and bottom panels from their height.

2. Fit your upright timbers to your base timber one at a time, initially drilling a pilot hole near the corners (use a countersunk drill bit) before adding wood glue along the end you're about to fix, then screw into place (the glue will make your finished piece far stronger).

3. Continue fixing it together at the sides and top. For larger pieces, add more supporting screws intermittently along the joins.

4. Screw on your castors (if using) and sand any rough edges. Decorate with wood paint, oil or varnish to suit your preferred look.

three projects to try

PROJECT ONE

PROJECT TWO

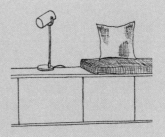

PROJECT THREE

Single seating cubes

Individual seating cubes on castors offer the ultimate flexible seating solution. This design has a lift-off top so you can use the internal space for storage, too. Adapt the steps (left) to create a four-sided box with a base, but instead of fitting the final length of wood to the top, leave it loose, then place some upholstery foam of the same size on its top side, wrap some fabric around it, then staple underneath.

By Lynsey Ford, Design Contestant, Series 2 episode 5

Workspace/ hangout seating

Convert your basic box bench into a dual-use workspace: fix on a taller back panel when constructing your seat, then use the other side to secure an additional shelf, supported on brackets. The seat's hollow interior can also be used for storage. If you like the natural look of birch ply, ensure you coat it with a matt protective oil at the end, to stop it yellowing in sunlight.

By Fran Lee and Paul Andrews, Design Contestants, Series 3, episode 3

Frank's built-in seating/shelving

For flexible storage and seating in an open-plan apartment, consider adding a row of fitted storage cubes or boxes that are around 45–50cm (18–19.5in) high: this height will allow them to double as extra seating when required (just throw on a couple of cushions to make them comfier). To make the storage accessible, you may need to work with a carpenter to create hinged tops or fold-down front panels.

By Frank Newbold, Design Contestant, Series 1, episode 8

Layout and colour

flexible quick fixes

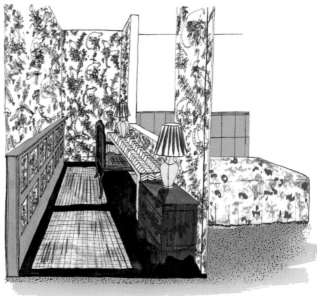

After something simpler? Try some of these ideas to help transform existing furniture into multi-use pieces:

- Add shelving to a cabinet or console table by placing a length of wood the same width as the cabinet's top, elevated on two sturdy risers. Cut-down wooden battens would do the job (and could be painted the same colour to blend them in), or, for an industrial style, try breeze blocks (as seen in Fran's window display in Series 3, episode 4).
- An upholstered ottoman instead of a coffee table can serve three different uses: storage, additional seating for unexpected guests, and as a coffee table (just keep a sturdy tray on its top).
- Look online for 'concertina' furniture, made from hard-wearing paper and cardboard, which allows you to transform something the size of a large book into lightweight stools or seating (as seen in Banjo and Molly's common room in Series 3, episode 3).

- Whether you're in a studio apartment or simply don't have much room to spare, a vertical wall bed (which you can fold up when not in use) frees up a lot of floor space for daytime activities like home working or exercising.
- For a fun, freestanding shelving alternative, take a double-sided wooden ladder and stand it open against a wall, then rest wooden boards on its steps (cut each board so it's slightly longer than the width between the two steps it's using as support). Drill the shelves into place through the step treads (like Micaela and Paul's display in Series 2, episode 4).

'Because of the size of Jon's room (see above), he's been able to pull the bed forward and pop a little dressing table area behind it, which is super effective because it allows the rest of the space to stay focused on the bed area and the view from the window.'

Michelle Ogundehin

super-small
vs super-sized

Whether your space is particularly bijou or cavernously large, both come with their own unique set of challenges. Here are some ideas on how you might handle them:

Super-small

- Add a slim shelf in front of a windowsill to turn it into more of a useable ledge, or even fit shelving across a window if it's one you don't ever open.
- Look out for modular storage furniture and containers, which can be pulled out to perform different functions but stored inside one another when not required.
- A fitted clothes rail could take up less space than a wardrobe within a bedroom (as well as working for guest rooms); use metal poles with socket end fittings to attach it to the wall and floor.
- Opting for wall-hung furniture leaves more of your flooring visible, which in turn helps smaller spaces feel larger as the eye is able to see a bigger footprint.

'I love small spaces. They present the ultimate design challenge and require loads of clever solutions: how can you fit everything you need into a small space and still make it look fabulous?'

Sophie Robinson, Interior Designer, Colour Expert and Guest Judge

Super-sized

- In a large bedroom, adding a false wall for your bedhead to go against creates a handy nook behind it for a walk-in wardrobe, or even an en suite.
- While high ceilings are generally considered desirable, those that are truly soaring might make it harder to feel cosy. To counter this, try optically lowering them by painting them (and possibly the top third of your walls, too) in a darker tone than the rest of the space.
- Scale up your furniture and accessories so that their size balances with the space. You may need to search for specialist suppliers online to get super-sized beds or sofas, or look at any commercial furniture dealers who might have bigger pieces intended for use in hotels and restaurants.
- Beware of spreading things out too thinly: it's better to group things together and deliberately leave corners bare for breathing space rather than scatter them about.

Colour

Colour is arguably one of the most important and impactful elements of any interiors scheme, and its use influences how we feel about a space regardless of whether you go for rainbow brights or all-out neutral. However, being such a crucial element, it can understandably cause anxiety if you're unsure of how to use it, or even of what you like – which in turn brings the risk of defaulting to playing it safe and potentially ending up with a space that doesn't quite please anyone.

The way our eyes perceive colour and the reasons why it makes us feel a certain way are fascinating and complex, but by getting to grips with a few basic concepts and principles you'll be able to develop the skills to make choices that work for you.

The colour wheel

While most of us will be familiar with the colour wheel, it's well worth revisiting it with an interiors mindset.

How does it work?

The basic colour wheel features three primary colours (red, yellow and blue), three secondary colours (green, orange and purple, which are each an equal mixture of the two adjacent primary colours), and six tertiary colours, which are tints and tones of both primary and secondary colours.

What are hues, tints and tones?

Hue refers to one of the six primary and secondary colours. Every individual colour has an underlying hue (aside from pure white, pure black and pure grey).

Tints are a variation of any colour lightened using white (essentially creating a paler version of the exact same colour).

Tones are a variation of any colour which has black or grey added to it, which creates both darker and more muted, nuanced and 'toned-down' colours.

How to combine colours

Going with your gut and working with colours you love is a brilliant approach, but it can be useful to understand some basic rules so you can bend or break them to suit your end goals. Based on the colour wheel, here are some key techniques:

Basic schemes:

- Monochromatic: a scheme that consists of a single hue, with both tints and tones of the same colour (a common misconception is that this only refers to black, white and grey, whereas the term applies to all hues). This makes for a very easy to live with look, albeit perhaps a little safe and dull.
- Analogous: next-door neighbours on the colour wheel, these can be thought

Analgous colours represent
those either side of one
segment of the colour wheel

of as harmonious due to their ability to sit well together. They bring a little more friction than a monochromatic scheme, but they hold back on the high drama.

\- Complementary: essentially contrasting colours, these hues sit opposite one another on the colour wheel, creating the most interesting (or overwhelming, depending on your viewpoint) colour schemes. You can, however, dial the drama up or down depending on which tints and tones you use: pillar-box red and bottle green are both opposites on the outer wheel, but if you work your way inwards, you'll find far softer tones of putty pink and sage green.

Colours within the two opposite,
complementary segments grow in saturation
and contrast the closer they get to the
outer edge

Getting more experimental:

\- A split-complementary colour palette pairs two analogous colours with the colour that's opposite the (unused) colour in between: for example, take purple

Monochromatic colours always live within
the same segment of the colour wheel

and red as your analogous colours and you'll find green sitting opposite. This combination brings both balance and contrast to a scheme.

- Dyadic and triadic colours bring together shades that are two spaces apart on the wheel, either using two (dyad) or three (triad) tones in total. The separation between each colour adds vibrancy and interest, yet each colour still has a degree of natural harmony with each other.

Identifying undertones

- Understanding the underlying dominant hue – the undertone – of any colour can really help you to nail your scheme. You might find you can tell at a glance: grass green is likely to have a visibly yellow undertone, whereas teal looks closer to the blue end of the spectrum. If in doubt, compare a 'true' hue next to any colours you're looking at to get a clearer idea of whether, say, the taupe paint you're eyeing up has a green or purple undertone. You should spot the tonal similarity when you put the right true hue next to your paint sample or material.

Warm or cool?

- If you're still unsure, stick with either cool or warm undertones. While the colour wheel is split into cool (purple/blue/green) and warm (yellow/orange/red), this needn't limit your colour choices: you can get a warm-toned blue, just as you can get cool-toned reds. Again, if in doubt, hold up a true hue against any colour to see whether a warm or cool hue looks to be present in its make-up.

- You needn't commit exclusively to all-warm or all-cold colours, but be mindful of which is dominant and how this works within your space. Warm colours generally work well in north-facing rooms and in colder climates, where the daylight tends to have a bluer tone, whereas cool colours are a good option for hot countries or very bright rooms.

'What Barbara's really got right is to take her lead for the palette from the wallpaper, but then she's been brave enough to throw in a vibrant contrast with pops of orange – and to use it consistently. Yes, you can have a bonkers wallpaper, but let that lead. Yes, you can throw in different patterns, but they must all have a narrative link.'

Michelle Ogundehin

BARBARA'S BOLD BEDROOM

With a brief outside of her comfort zone, Barbara's hotel room makeover in Series 2, episode 3 offers a masterclass on the application of a key rule when it comes to balancing colours: go with 60% of the dominant colour as your main tone (in this instance, saturated blue); use 30% of a second colour in a supportive role (here, it's harmonising green, picked out from the wallpaper and mirrored in the bedlinen); then add in 10% of a complementary colour to act as an accent (the orange).

'She's taken the wallpaper all the way up to the ceiling to stop it feeling bitty, then taken the softer blue tone from the paper onto the ceiling so it's not too oppressive. She's then got the below-dado area in a Kingfisher blue that picks out the tones of the wallpaper well, and there's also the blue of the carpet, which gives an overall jewel-box effect.'

Kit Kemp, *Interior Designer and Guest Judge*

what's your colour personality?

Before delving too deeply into the properties of individual colours, it's useful to view them collectively from a psychological perspective. One way in which many experts do this is by splitting tints and tones into four seasonally inspired palettes which represent not only the colours of that season, but also its mood and energy.

Many of us find we resonate more strongly with one seasonal palette, or discover we have a primary and secondary palette; homing in on which yours might be can help take the stress out of many decorating decisions, and ultimately help you produce a scheme that's both cohesive and suits your personality.

advice from the experts: how to get to grips with seasonal colour psychology

By Sophie Robinson, Interior Designer, Colour Expert and Guest Judge

Colour psychology is a huge, fascinating topic, and it's a framework I follow when teaching my online students. Here's how I use it to create a feeling in a space, not just a 'look':

Joyful & uplifting

Mood: a time of rebirth and new growth, the spring season represents optimism, youthful energy, joy and positivity, with a 'busy' energy.
Palette: joyful shades are 'clear' colours - containing no black; this keeps them feeling fresh and buoyant. Pastel shades typify this palette due to their lightness, punctuated by energising colours such as coral red and yellow.
Motifs and materials: ditsy florals, small-scale prints, lightweight linens, reflective surfaces, pale woods, trend-led designs.
Must-have: lots of natural light.
Good for: social and creative spaces for a welcoming yet modern feel.

Graceful & calm

Mood: inspired by summer - think breezy hay meadows and leisurely picnics rather than flamingos and pineapple prints. Summer's vibe offers a laid-back antidote to the perkier spring energy.
Palette: as flowers droop in full

bloom and everything becomes sun-bleached and faded, we see more dusty, powdery tones (think hydrangeas and roses). Summer shades share cooler grey and blue-based undertones for a calming effect.

Motifs and materials: tactile fabrics (think cashmere and French linen), elegant fluid shapes, weathered finishes, a sense of symmetry and restraint, classic designs (with a focus more on materiality than pattern).

Must-have: fitted storage.

Good for: areas you want to feel relaxed, calm and orderly, like bedrooms and formal dining rooms.

Grounded & cosy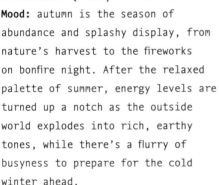

Mood: autumn is the season of abundance and splashy display, from nature's harvest to the fireworks on bonfire night. After the relaxed palette of summer, energy levels are turned up a notch as the outside world explodes into rich, earthy tones, while there's a flurry of busyness to prepare for the cold winter ahead.

Palette: colours are deep, rich, earthy and punchy – think leaves turning vibrant russet red, and grasses moving from green to auburns and golds. Autumn colours always have a warm yellow undertone, with a tint of black which makes them feel grounded (you won't find cool tones in a true autumnal palette).

Motifs and materials: maximalist heritage prints (think William Morris), textural velvets, rough-hewn woods, craftsmanship, rustic and robust finishes.

Must-have: a roaring fire.

Good for: casual and cosy rooms which you want to feel both welcoming and inviting, such as living spaces, libraries and snugs.

Impactful & striking

Mood: winter is a time of extremes – think of the stark contrast of bare branches set against barren, dramatic landscapes. Autumn's blazing energy makes way for a stiller, cooler look, punctuated by strong silhouettes and a more minimal landscape.

Palette: impactful, striking and strong – winter colours are saturated and, set in contrast against one another, make a statement. The only palette to feature the true primary colours alongside pure black and pure white, all winter tones share a cold undertone and are high-contrast hues, featuring bold brights like acid yellow and Ferrari red.

Motifs and materials: striking and impressive with no unnecessary ornamentation. Luxury, stark materials (think marble, leather and high-shine metals). Iconic designer accessories and modern art pieces create a bold statement in an otherwise slick, fuss-free scheme.

Must-have: the latest home tech.

Good for: open-plan apartments designed to impress, super-sized bedroom suites and double-height entrance spaces for some wintry wow.

Individual colour tones

focus on: **green**

Green is generally considered a very easy colour to live with, but the reasons why might surprise you. As well as being the colour we tend to associate most with nature and its related health benefits, it's a hue that sits right in the middle of the visible spectrum of colours our eyes can see – meaning we find it the easiest to read and process. These facts combined make it a good choice for any room you'd like to feel grounded, soothing and balanced. It's also the colour that contains more variation than any other, so if you're keen to bring its calming benefits into your home, there's bound to be at least one tint or tone that suits whatever scheme you're looking to create.

Properties

Said to symbolise new beginnings (think verdant shoots emerging at the start of spring), studies have shown that just looking at the colour green can lead to more creative ideas than blue, red or grey. Depending on its tone, it can leave you feeling invigorated and refreshed, grounded and relaxed, or comforted and cocooned. You can, however, have too much of a good thing: the phrase 'green with envy' is believed to originate from green's association with fearfulness and jealousy, and it's thought that surrounding yourself with too much green can lead to feelings of stagnation.

Cassie was praised for her immersive mix of greens in her barber's shop redesign in Series 1, episode 7

How to use it

Sitting on the boundary between cool and warm on the colour wheel, warmer greens will generally have a yellow undertone (think olive, chartreuse and pistachio) while cooler hues like teal, emerald and forest will have a blue undertone. Stick to all-warm or all-cool colours for a more harmonious palette, or, if you'd like to add in some friction, mix them up: for example, pair a warm moss-green wall with a blue-hued emerald accent. With such a varied spectrum, there's a great green for any circumstance – from muted non-stimulating shades for a bedroom to bolder, immersive applications to give a sense of blurred lines between indoors and out.

Three ways with green

-   Green undertones often form the basis of warm neutral schemes: muted tones of laurel leaf or sea mist can add subtle greenery to a pared-back space for a tranquil feel. A warmer minty hue can work well with a brown-toned neutral, for a fresh yet earthy look.

-   Green can bring some punchy drama if you go for deep, saturated tones such as malachite, emerald or bottle green. Introduce a dash of contrasting red or orange, or harmonise with blue: an equal dark will give an intriguing wraparound feel, or lighten things up with a paler tint.

-   Poppy, impactful, blue-toned greens such as mint and turquoise can feel fresh and invigorating; playing up this fun vibe with other pastel and sorbet tones can feel youthful and energetic, but, to avoid a saccharine end result, bring in tones that contain a dash of grey or keep it within a more mature, monochromatic palette.

Layout and colour

focus on:
blue

A number of surveys over the years have revealed blue to be the world's most popular colour, and there are multiple reasons behind this: we tend to associate most things that are blue as being either positive or neutral rather than negative, and blue is also the tone found most readily in nature. Yet historically it's been a difficult hue to reproduce, giving it an air of desirability and mystique which remains associated with it today, despite technology now allowing us to readily recreate it in any tone we wish.

Properties

Like its colour-wheel companion green, blue's connection to nature brings with it a sense of calmness and serenity, and it is even said to aid clarity of thought. Depending on how it's used (both the shades you choose and the spaces it's used in), it can feel uplifting or rejuvenating – but on the flip side, it runs the risk of feeling physically cold and uninviting (as per the phrase, 'feeling blue'). As such, it's even more important to be aware of whether the blues you're considering have cold or warm undertones, and also whether the light in your space is north or south facing; to avoid ending up with a room that feels unwelcoming, choose warm-toned shades unless you're in a bright, south-facing space.

How to use it

From the deepest inky indigo to the palest hint of duck egg, blue runs a wide gamut. Residing firmly on the cool side of the colour wheel, the key to stopping blue feeling too cold is to choose the right undertone and intensity to match the feeling you want to evoke. Pairing it with its complementary colours of reds and oranges can help to turn up the heat a little, while sticking with neighbouring colours green and purple will generally give a more serene feeling.

tip

Do you have any long-held prejudices against certain colours? Think carefully about this one - it's something we're not always consciously aware of. If you find certain shades make you shudder, this could be connected to a memory from the past, and figuring this out could help you confront it and even change your perceptions.

Charlotte went for full impact in her Series 2, episode 1 bedroom redesign creating both a feature wall and artwork in the same bold, inky tone, tempering it with cool white elsewhere in the space

Three ways with blue

- If you like dark interiors, a rich indigo can have more depth than a straight-up grey (and be less harsh than black), thanks to its warmer violet or red undertones, depending on the exact colour. Minty greens can pop beautifully against it, while cool titanium white provides contrast.

- Ultramarine is a great choice for a punchy, uplifting scheme - for energetic, sociable spaces, consider teaming it with a warm yellow and purpley-pinks (if this feels too strong, opt for paler tints of these tones).

- To evoke the feeling of a classic seascape oil painting, bring in a palette of blues that are all tonally similar, utilising monochromatic and analogous colours. Blues with violet and yellow undertones will give the look a lift.

focus on:
red & pink

While reds and pinks have typically been considered feminine and even 'sexy' colours, this social conditioning has been quietly shifting in recent years, with the huge popularity of genderless 'Millennial pink' (a muted blush shade with beige undertones) giving pink's image something of a makeover. Increasingly, pinks are cropping up as a 'new neutral' in interiors, and are making their way into communal spaces such as hallways and living areas. Essentially a tint of red, pink tones tend to provide 'watered-down' effects compared to full-on red tones: while red represents passion, pink is more empathic and nurturing. Red shouts at us to look at it, while also acting as a warning, while pink asks more gently, but can appear submissive.

Richard opted for a warm, peachy-pink as a base neutral in his Series 3, episode 1 bedroom design, adding accents of earthy red in his mural art and a flash of cobalt blue on his headboard

Properties

The stereotype of men psychologically finding women who wear red more sexually attractive has been supported in studies; though pink also has its own superpowers, with other studies revealing that immersing yourself in a pink space can lower individual aggression levels. As well as eliciting feelings of lust, red is also viewed as a strong, courageous, energetic tone, though if it's used too heavily it can feel like too much and deplete your energy levels. Pink offers more nuance, with a far greater range of tones – from sickly-sweet sugary hues, which can feel very gendered, to punchier brights, which read as more subversive and powerful.

How to use it

While its lusty connotations can make red seem like a good option for bedrooms, use with caution: it could equally stir up arguments or create an environment that is unconducive to sleep, so it's best kept to smaller accents. Be aware that it's not really a colour you can turn off, so while it might seem like a good idea for sparking conversation in a dining room, perhaps contain it to removable elements like table linen and crockery. Warm-toned neutral pinks can work well as both a main and accent colour in most spaces, though more vibrant shades that move closer to red are best used with more caution.

Three ways with pink and red

- Outdated fashion rules decreed that pink and red should never be used together, though actually this combination can work wonderfully both in clothing and interiors. For a bold look, pair a pillar-box red with a bold blue-hued magenta, or, for something visually softer, use an orange-toned red with a paler pink.

- Another outmoded saying, 'red and green should never be seen', does come with a kernel of truth: these complementary tones, if both used at a high intensity, can be quite overwhelming; but if the green is a pale sage, and you mix in a pale neutral for balance, you get a far less intense palette.

- Pink also proves a wonderful foil for green. To stop a pale, dusky pink feeling too sweet, ground it with a warm, earthy olive and add a flash of deep burgundy as an accent.

focus on:
orange & yellow

Taking the intensity down a notch from reds, oranges and yellows are arguably among the happiest shades on the colour wheel, sitting firmly on the warmer side of the spectrum. Associated with heat and warmth, it's long been known that our exposure to bright sunlight (and the lack of it during winter months) directly impacts our mood and health. But even without the sun, studies have shown that exposure to bright, orange-hued light can have positive effects on our circadian rhythms (the body's internal clock), so it stands to reason that simply surrounding ourselves with these mellow, comforting tones can help bring a little mental health boost, too.

Properties

Yellow, a mixture of red and green, shares many of the same properties as orange and can have wonderfully uplifting properties, yet there can be too much of a good thing; using it liberally and at a strong intensity can result in a space that feels uncomfortable to be in for too long due to the amount of light yellow reflects. While orange brings a lively, almost cheeky warmth, its own downside is it can feel cheap and frivolous if not handled with care.

How to use it

Although these are ultimately warm colours, some shades of orange and yellow still have cool grey or green undertones, which can give them a fresher, more restrained hue than richer, earthy shades with brown undertones. Think zesty lemons compared to auburn-toned autumnal falling leaves. Use bold yellows sparingly – they can be a good option for transient spaces like a hallway, to give you a passing

Amy's bold retro basement bar (Series 3, episode 8) featured an orange and yellow patterned wallpaper that was tempered with a black background

hit of uplifting colour. Softer terracotta tones can be used more as a grounding neutral in a broader range of areas, but, as with red, keep any very vibrant shades to pops, unless you're aiming for an intense, invigorating scheme.

'The trouble with the colour orange is it's very divisive – when some people think of orange, they think zesty and fresh, but to other people they think budget airlines and fake tan.'

Alan Carr, Presenter, Interior Design Masters

Three ways with orange and yellow

- Vibrant tangerine tones became popular in the 1960s and 70s; recreate this playful retro palette by pairing it with cyan blue and bold red accents.

- Create a harmonious yet liveable orange and yellow palette by opting for a warm peach as your dominant colour, ground it with a darker terracotta, and throw in some light sorbet yellow for a dramatic accent.

- For a contemporary look, temper coral tones with a warm French grey. An addition of dark navy will give added sophistication.

focus on:
purple

While purple is technically a manufactured colour, created from equal quantities of blue and red, indigo and violet (which sit within this bracket) are 'true' colours that are found in nature. The colour purple has long-standing links to wealth and luxury; traditionally it was costly to reproduce, so became the preserve of only royalty and the very rich. Violet, however, is the colour most associated with spirituality, due to it having the shortest wavelength in our visible spectrum (hence its connection to the universe and higher realms). Whatever your beliefs, this colour family is said to encourage contemplation, help us connect to our intuition, and even encourage bold, creative thinking.

Micaela's cafe seating area in Series 2, episode 7 mixed soft pastel tones of mint green and peach with a grey-tinted lilac

Properties

As a colour our eyes naturally find somewhat difficult to process, it can be a polarising, love-it-or-hate-it hue – and if surrounded with too much of it, its contemplative qualities can also run the risk of causing us to become withdrawn. Sitting on the cool side of the colour wheel, the somewhat garish purple tones favoured a decade or two ago mainly featured cooler blue undertones, yet in recent years its popularity has grown as it's moved towards more grounded, complex inky palettes. On the lighter end of the scale, lilac and lavender tones have been making headlines in the design world, with 'digital lavender' – a grey-toned pale lilac – being referred to as a 'zeitgeist-defining pigment' which reflects the blurring of our online existence with reality. These paler hues still contain the power of purple, but are both visually and metaphorically lighter.

How to use it

If you favour dark bedrooms, consider a warm violet as an alternative to dark grey or navy for a softer, more cocooning feel. With its links to creativity and open-mindedness, it can be a great option for a home study space, craft room, or even a kitchen if you're keen to get more experimental with your cooking. If you are spiritually minded, it's also a natural choice for a relaxing, meditative nook or home yoga studio.

Three ways with purple

- Introduce a little visual friction by teaming cool-toned lilac with warm-toned coral, then add in some pale blue for a fresh, icy look.

- For a warmer, heritage feel, bring in a rich, deep damson and add some drama with gold accents. A red-toned beetroot will provide complementary layering for a harmonious feel.

- Landscape artists tend to use dark violet tones instead of black or grey to add shadows to sunlit scenes. Borrow this technique and combine warm sunshine yellows with earthy greens, and add dashes of deep violet as a rich accent.

focus on:
black & darks

The move towards boldly decorating our homes with black and dark colours has been spearheaded by designers like guest judge Abigail Ahern over the last decade, and it's a trend that remains popular, but it's not for everyone – even if you objectively like the look. Greys and blacks can almost be thought of as non-colours, which has both positive and negative connotations. They can offer the perfect antidote to a busy life (or busy mind), helping to minimise any visual or mental clutter without distraction – but on the downside, this lack of stimulus could then leave your mind to ruminate.

Properties

Outside of pure black, greys and dark hues can contain a broad range of different tints and tones for a non-colour. From cool-toned concretes to warmer brown-hued charcoals, it's possible to create dramatically different looks between colours which may, at first glance, not appear all that dissimilar from one another. Dark tones will absorb the light within the room, creating a very different feeling to an all-white space: when this is positively received, it can feel safe and protective, and even empowering, but it also risks being oppressive if it feels at odds with your mood and personality. It can feel like you're choosing to hibernate from the world – which for some may sound like heaven, for others closer to hell.

How to use it

A 'go hard or go home' approach is good to take when it comes to dark interiors, so if you're up for the former, opt for a 'colour drenching' effect, where you paint walls, ceilings, woodwork and even floors all in the same dark hue. While this may sound extreme, visually it blurs the boundaries within a room and can help small spaces appear larger as the room's definitions are effectively eliminated. If you have limited (or north-facing) natural light, painting everything dark can conversely help it to feel cosier and more intimate, but balance this out by sticking with hues that have a warm, rich undertone.

If this sounds too extreme, use dark tones sparingly to visually zone off a cosy nook within an otherwise busy space. Or, work with lighter and darker tints of the same shade, so you don't have wraparound dark but there's still a nod to the effect.

'To give some shape and character to a black room and stop it feeling flat, put up some dado rails or panelling. When I want to create a dark scheme, if I don't use pure black I'll generally go with a charcoal, which is a little softer, or a black with a yellow or red base tone, for warmth. I don't really use grey as I think it often feels like a compromise, plus only certain colours pop with grey, whereas with black there are more options.'

Dean Powell, Design Contestant, Series 3

Jerome's crisp black and white hotel bedroom (Series 1, episode 2) was softened with dark forest green fabric accents, to stop it feeling too austere

Three ways with blacks and darks

- Black is a brilliant way to temper more 'immature' hues, like ice-cream pastel shades, but opt for a tint with a warm undertone so it doesn't give too much of a visual jolt.

- Team deep black with equally rich, colourful tones – like mustard and raspberry – for it to play off for a powerful scheme. For a more tonal look, make your 'black' a deep, dark saturation of your lighter accent, such as pairing raspberry with a red-toned dark mulberry.

- For a moody twist on a nature-inspired palette, pair a nearly-black, deep forest green with some stronger olive tones, then bring in a violet-toned lighter grey to represent the sky at dusk.

focus on:
white & light neutral tones

Surprisingly, although tonally in total contrast to black and dark spaces, white and light colours in interiors can come with the same set of challenges. Depending on the hues you choose, just like black and grey they can be something of a non-colour; this can be a blessing if you're after a clean, simple feel, but equally they run the risk of looking like you just didn't get round to choosing a palette. That's not to say neutrals are a lazy choice – a well-executed neutral scheme can be challenging to pull off at times – more that it's important to consciously choose them, rather than letting them choose you.

Cassie's student bedroom bunk (Series 1, episode 4) utilsed the natural warmth of birch ply against pale ivory walls, with a turmeric-toned bed linen set to tie everything together

Properties

It's a common misconception that pure brilliant white works with everything – it's actually a rather cold and unforgiving tone that is best suited to warm, sunny climates and spaces that receive lots of south-facing sunshine. Certainly, in the UK, a light colour with a warm undertone, or a pale-but-still-interesting hue, can feel more welcoming and less clinical.

There are no real rules as to what constitutes a neutral, but generally

Three ways with neutrals

- A little pop of yellow can add an uplift against a warm beige (aim for brown undertones in both). Bringing in a yellow-based green like chartreuse will give extra interest.

- Black and white always looks classic, but to avoid it feeling stark try a chalky white with a hint of yellow undertone, opposite a brown-black. An accent of terracotta adds depth while retaining the overall classical feel.

- Greige (unsurprisingly a mixture of grey and beige) can be considered a warm neutral, but it tends to have cool green undertones. Mixing in a leafy green can help bring this out, while adding in some pale grey accents gives it a contemporary air.

speaking in decorating it's used in reference to lighter tones of greys and blues, beiges and creams, taupes and putty tones, and – increasingly – pinks. The paler the colour, the more light it reflects into our eyes, allowing us to spot subtle variations in tone more easily than very dark hues. Therefore, it's especially important to be aware of the undertones in any colours you choose, and consider ways you can bring in warmth if you're opting for a cooler palette.

How to use it

By definition, neutrals tend to work in a variety of spaces and settings, so it really does come down to how you want the space to feel. Might a crisp white living room feel oppressive and uninspiring to you, or would it offer the perfect antidote to busy family life? It's particularly

important to try and bring a feeling of warmth and comfort into more private spaces like bedrooms and bathrooms, where you'll be undressing and bathing, to help you feel comfortable during moments of physical vulnerability.

'While dark and bright colours tend to advance – making your room feel more intimate – light and dim colours tend to recede, and open up your space.'

Ju De Paula, Design Contestant, Series 1

4

Essential components

'Interior design is ultimately about seduction... having a great idea in two dimensions is lovely, but our job is about creating loveliness in three dimensions.'

Laurence Llewelyn-Bowen, Interior Designer and Guest Judge

Lighting and ambiance

decorating for the senses

Before diving into the nitty-gritty of fundamentals such as flooring, fixtures and fittings, there's an almost undefinable element that's often overlooked yet is integral to the overall success of your final space: ambiance, and the idea of decorating for all five senses.

Of course, interior design always focuses heavily on sight, but how much thought have you given to the other elements that play a part in helping your house feel like a home? Together, they combine to create a certain feel, mood and energy – and this will happen both with and without your input, so it's worth focusing on the other four.

Smell

Our brains process scent in a similar way to memory, meaning we can have a visceral, mood-altering response to certain aromas. Candles, incense sticks and oil burners can all be used to powerfully alter the vibe of your space, so choose carefully depending on how you want to feel – a calming lavender room spray is a great option for a night-time wind-down or, to counter a mid-afternoon slump, try a blast of peppermint through a diffuser.

Sound

If areas of your home are echoey, it can subconsciously leave you feeling disconcerted; bringing in natural materials, like a wall of plants or real wood cladding, can help dull it down. Consider using partition screens to section off a quiet area for improved acoustics.

Touch

Think about the 'tactile journey' around your space: what's happening under your feet? Which materials can your hands brush against as you pass them? While you needn't feel obliged to decorate with lots of carpets and textiles if you prefer a sleek look, bear in mind that spaces without a modicum of textural softness can feel uncomfortably stark.

Taste

While licking your walls is inadvisable, 'taste' can be interpreted less literally: just like choosing a meal, do you want a space that is warm and comforting, or fresh and light? What elements from the other senses could help achieve this?

expert comments

'It's hard to create ambience. It has to come from a place of passion.'

Michelle Ogundehin

'For me, interior design is about creating a fantasy, a safe haven, an unforgettable experience. It's about how objects, colours and lights – or the lack of these – make you feel. It's the emotional response to the physical world that excites me.'

Linda Boronkay, Interior Designer and Guest Judge

'In restaurant design, the food is just the tip of the iceberg: the ambiance, the decor and the way the space makes you feel is of paramount importance. You want to feel good in the light of that space, but it's got to have that level of practicality, and it's got to look pretty.'

Nisha Katona, Chef, Restaurateur and Guest Judge

This layered living room space Paul designed for his holiday home makeover in Series 3, episode 7 plays with multiple textures and materials

Essential components

what are your lighting options?

Lighting is an essential, functional aspect of any home – but when it comes to thinking like an interior designer, it does a whole lot more than simply help us get from A to B without tripping over. Used as a design tool, it can help to create a mood, be that eliciting calm or ramping up the drama, while ensuring it's fulfilling the practical requirements of each resident.

Lighting types

Before you get started with any plans, it's key to understand the different types of lighting, what they do and how to utilise them. Broadly speaking, they will fall under one of three categories – your job is working out what type you need where, and whether to layer these different types together, or stick to a single source.

Ambient

By definition, 'ambient' light comes from all directions. Think of this as the 'general', no-nonsense functional light required to illuminate a whole space so you can see where you are and what you're doing. In most rooms, this would be the overhead light. While this is usually a first port of call when the sun goes down, many interior designers are 'anti-big-light' as its practicality is also a bit of a mood killer.

Task

Performing a purely practical job, task lighting is usually used in corners and nooks where the ambient light isn't enough. In a home workspace or craft corner, an angled table lamp is often the best option, while a reading nook could benefit from a softer treatment, such as a standard lamp with an evenly dispersed light more conducive to relaxation. As any Instagrammer knows, a 'ring of light' is the most even and flattering for the face, so take this into account around bathroom and dressing table mirrors.

Accent

A light source where you can play more with mood and ambiance (which, despite sounding similar, means something a little different to 'ambient' when it comes to lighting). Accent lighting is, by nature, supplementary to task and ambient light: without it, you'd still be able to function perfectly well within the space, but it'd likely feel flat and uninviting. Think of accent lighting as the seasoning in your cooking; although it might not be the main element of the meal, without it you're likely to be left with something that's a bit bland. It can be used to bring drama – such as a tailored light beam on a particular area – or act as a layered background element, like a string of LED lights along a mantlepiece for a bit of ambient twinkle.

a note on spotlights

Depending on how they're used, these can act as either ambient or task lighting. If dotted evenly over a ceiling, they'd qualify as the former, though take care to avoid going overboard and calculate that sweet spot between good illumination vs airport hangar aesthetics. As a general rule of thumb, divide your ceiling height by two to work out the ideal spacing between lights (so a ceiling height of 3m/10 ft would benefit from spotlight spacing of 1.5 m/5 ft per spot). For tasks, ensure you have some in areas where shadows might otherwise hinder what you're doing, such as over a kitchen sink or hob, or underneath wall units where you're likely to be prepping food.

up or down?

+   Uplights are specifically designed to send a beam or wash of light upwards, creating dramatic shadows and drawing the eye towards the ceiling (a useful trick for small rooms with high ceilings, as it can visually fool you into perceiving the overall space as bigger than it is).

+   Downlights, unsurprisingly, do the same job in reverse, and are particularly useful for highlighting artworks or throwing light down into corners the main ceiling light never quite reaches. They can also provide a more practical light source, illuminating the floor (useful in spaces that may have steps or sharp corners, for example).

'Every space I create is really about the people that use it, how they use it, and how they feel when they're in it ... I'm thinking about all the different senses, the touch, the vision, the warmth of the colours that you use, so when they walk in there, they feel something.'

Lynsey Ford, Design Contestant, Series 2

'Natural and artificial lighting are in constant conversation with one another – our job is to engage in this conversation and manipulate them respectively in the best way we see fit. Artificial light is introduced as a second layer that will direct your eyeline to key features in the room, or encourage you to look up or remain low in a space. Each decision made has consequential affects on the feeling and look of a space.'

Buse Gurbuz, Design Contestant, Series 4

setting a mood

Just as using bold stripes of paint or wallpaper can visually define different areas of a room, so too can lighting. Think of it as a tool to help you zone out a space, drawing attention to the best bits and allowing other areas to (literally) sink into the shadows. And while insufficient lighting for practical tasks can cause eye strain and hinder concentration, likewise if it doesn't strike the right tone it can leave you feeling unable to relax and even inhibit sleep.

Assess all the different ways you use your space, and determine your differing requirements. Yes, you need to see clearly in the bathroom when you're trying to avoid dribbling toothpaste down your top, but when it comes to enjoying a relaxing soak in the tub, gentler, less intrusive lighting will be more conducive to spa vibes.

Where possible, include several lighting sources in your room which tick off all the requirements of ambient, task and accent lighting. You might need to get creative on how to achieve this in certain rooms, such as the bathroom, where lamps are obviously a no-no: opting for a mains light on a dimmer (with the socket sited just outside the room), and switching to candles and SELV (safety extra low voltage) LED lighting strips for relaxation times could work around this issue.

A mix of woven shades and bare bulbs brought warmth to Banjo's industrial bar space in Series 3, episode 8

Lighting that supports our circadian rhythm (our natural 24-hour cycle) is a crucial part of self-care and also helps with sleep hygiene. Warmer, red-toned lights can help you wind down in the evening, whereas a stronger, blue-toned white light will get you going in the morning.

Vintage tungsten-style bulbs (which now come with slim LED strips in place

advice from the experts:
how to layer your lighting

By Abigail Ahern, Interior Designer and Guest Judge

+ Where you can, make sure all your ceiling lights are on dimmers, so you can change the vibe of your room by lowering the lighting levels.

+ I love accent lighting, and I use lamps everywhere: on side tables, consoles, kitchen islands, on the floor – even on a pouffe. These little glowing pockets of light create atmospheric, intimate spaces; enter a beautifully lit room and you immediately get that feeling of contentment. Battery-powered LED lights mean you can add them to places you couldn't plug in a normal lamp.

+ Don't forget candles: they're one of the easiest and most effective ways of adding an intriguing glow to a room. Make sure you have several clusters at different heights to create a warm atmosphere with oodles of depth.

+ Although I'm a fan of using lots of different light sources, don't eradicate all shadows completely. It's the contrast between the light and shadow that makes all the magic happen – and will make the biggest difference to your space.

of traditional carbon filaments) work well for the former: good looking enough to leave 'naked', their gentle glow is easy on the eye and great for creating a calming atmosphere. With lower kelvins (a scale that determines a bulb's light output), they may be a little too dim for passing areas such as hallways. For more practical ambient lighting, especially where the bulb won't be prominent, choose a bulb with higher kelvins for a brighter light that more closely mimics daylight: a clear glass bulb will give out a crisper light, though if this feels a little harsh, try a frosted bulb instead, which acts as a diffuser. Mirrored

bulbs pair well with a reflective or mirrored shade for optimum light bounce.

'The Soho bar I designed for episode 8 had an identity crisis – I wanted to make sure the separate spaces spoke the same design language, and I realised that what I needed to create was more of a mood. Lighting was very important in this – I knew I needed to bring that down to create a warmer kind of space.'

Banjo Beale, Design Contestant, Series 3

lighting 101

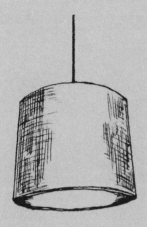 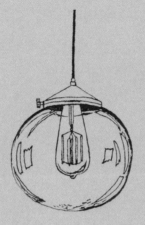 

Solid shades

Whether made from fabric, metal, ceramics or another material, light will be funnelled downwards, which can create an atmospheric effect. Be mindful that the colour of the shade will influence the hue it casts.

Clear shades

Glass or Perspex fittings will allow the light to spread more evenly throughout the room, and could be a better option for naturally dark spaces where the lights need to be left on during gloomy days. Bear in mind with clear lights that the bulb will be fully visible, so it's worth getting a good-looking one.

Diffused shades

Often used in kitchens and bathrooms (where moisture levels and proximity to water can be an issue), these frosted, fluted or textured shades can be used to bring softness to any room.

Keen to try customising your own shades and bases? Pages 228–229 have some projects to try at home.

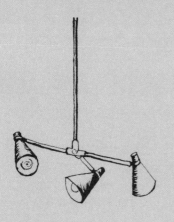

Chandeliers and multi-arm lamps

Good choices for spreading light throughout all corners of the room. For bigger spaces, or those with gloomy corners, opt for designs with multi-arms which can be angled, so you can adjust exactly where the light goes.

Rise-and-fall pendants

A flexible option, these lights allow you to alter the mood as required. Best used above fixed furniture such as a dining table, they can be dropped down low for an intimate dinner, or raised high for more general ambient light.

Clamp lights

Can be invaluable for small or tricky spaces which require a lighting boost. Clip them onto shelving for an uplighting effect, or in bedrooms with no space for a bedside table, attach one to your headboard or bedframe instead.

Get lighting smart

+ Harness technology to work in your favour: install simple lighting motion sensors inside cupboard doors, or opt for a smart lightbulb which you can control with your smartphone.

+ Be mindful of heights: a short or small pendant light hung from a very tall ceiling can look visually 'off', but going too low can be a head-hitting hazard (unless it's over a fixed piece of furniture like a dining table or breakfast bar).

+ To match or mismatch? If you've got a small space, or you prefer a very cohesive look, opt for the same styles of lighting design across ceiling, floor and table lamps. But if you prefer a more organic, layered aesthetic, mix in different styles but choose one unifying element - such as colour or material - or group them together so they don't feel disparate.

Flooring

how to visually define a space

Flooring is a fundamental element of your home design. So, if you're renovating a room from scratch, it's important to consider the general treatment you're going to go for during the first-fix stage to ensure you've got the correct sub-floor in place before deciding on specific colours and materials.

Material choices

TYPE	BEST FOR
Cork	Natural, biophilic schemes (cork has impeccable eco credentials).
Carpet	Softening the acoustics of an echoey space; providing comfort in places you might often be barefoot, like bedrooms.
Engineered wood	Bringing the beauty of real wood into your home (engineered planks are finished with a layer of real wood veneer on top of a manufactured base).
Laminate wood	Low budgets, or for a broader range of colours and finishes than real wood comes in (laminate planks feature a high-resolution facsimile print, so can be visually manipulated).
Porcelain tiles	Areas where the material they are mimicking (such as marble or concrete) wouldn't be practically appropriate.
Natural material tiles	Bringing earthy, natural variation: quarry, terracotta, slate and brick contain warmth and character, but generally require more maintenance than their porcelain counterparts.

restore old floors

+ If you're in a period property, there might be some beautiful original floorboards lurking beneath any current dubious flooring choices. Original planks are usually easy to replace if the odd one is damaged, and if you sand and stain (or paint) everything in the same finish, you won't really be able to tell the difference between old and new.

+ Save your sawdust while sanding: it can be mixed with PVA glue and used to fill floorboard gaps, which works wonderfully, as the PVA has a little flex in it so will cope with the movement in the boards.

+ If you like the patina and character of old wood floors but want a fresher look, use a traditional stain or limewash to lighten things up.

While these options will range wildly in price, depending on your final choice of material and finish, generally speaking 'fake' materials (such as laminate, vinyl and porcelain) will be cheaper than the real-life materials they often mimic, though they can also be less environmentally friendly. Weigh up both your budget and each product's sustainability before making a purchase.

Which way to lay?

- Laying tiles or boards on a 45-degree diagonal angle can help the space feel larger: it tricks the eye as it doesn't follow the boundaries of the room.

- Horizontal boards help a narrow space feel wider, as the eye is drawn along the space.
- Vertical boards lead the eye through the room, giving it depth. They work well in semi-open layouts, visually leading you through and into any outside space.

In smaller areas, go for larger format tiles or planks (and skip any decorative borders, too): it reads as less busy, so the space appears larger and less cluttered. Smaller spaces can also benefit from using the same flooring throughout, to visually remove boundaries that different flooring types tend to create.

'Spend the most you can possibly afford on your flooring – if you've got a rubbish floor, it will taint everything sat upon it.'

Michelle Ogundehin

make it bespoke

Replacing existing flooring can be a costly and complicated job, especially if it involves additional work on your subfloor in order to ensure your new flooring material is sound. And if you're renting, your landlord likely won't want you to touch such fundamental elements.

There are plenty of workarounds, however, if you're stuck with a flooring you don't like but can't (or don't want to) replace in a conventional way:

Play with paint

Not all flooring can be painted, but your options could be wider than you realise. Solid wood flooring is arguably the easiest surface to deal with, simply requiring a sand and clean first before applying paint or stain suitable for floorboards. Yet if you use the right paint (and do the right prep), you can also paint most tiles, concrete, and even linoleum flooring: check with your local DIY store to see what paint options are suitable for your specific circumstance.

Try:

- Using a band of colour on the floor to signpost in a certain direction to aid the overall flow of the space, like Banjo's bold orange floor stripe within his bar entrance in Series 3, episode 8, which encouraged guests to follow it into the main space.
- Stencilling a design on top of a painted floor to bring in a bespoke pattern (search online for designs, or create your own by cutting a pattern out of acetate).
- Splatter painting: paint the flooring with one all-over colour first, then use a semi-dry brush with your accent colour(s) to gently flick paint onto the floor, creating a New England-inspired speckled look.

Work with wood

For an affordable take on the industrial look, try laying sheets of inexpensive wood such as ply or OSB (fixed with screws or nails, depending on what you're attaching it to). It can be painted using floor paint for wood (depending on your look) or simply left au naturel, but it will quickly scuff so it's wise to seal with a clear matte floor varnish. In new-build properties, check what's under your existing carpet or laminate floor – you might find there's a suitably industrial-style sub-floor or solid wood underlay already in place.

Clever cover-ups

It's possible to lay wood-style laminate flooring planks directly on top of existing floors (though you may need to sandwich underlay between the layers): it can even be done without directly gluing or fixing it to the sub-floor, making it an option for renters. Another renter-friendly measure is to lay vinyl sheet flooring on top of existing flooring, securing it in place using double-sided carpet tape so you can remove it when required. As vinyl is water-resistant and easy to cut, it works especially well in bathrooms and kitchens.

Creative configurations

-   Use alternate coloured laminate flooring planks to create a contemporary twist on the chequerboard tile, like Nicki and Frank did in their restaurant space in Series 1, episode 6 (shown left).
-   Peel-and-stick tiles are easy to apply and offer more flexibility for creating a custom look. Play with colours to create unusual arrangements, or even cut into them with a specialist lino knife to produce gentle curves and patterns.
-   Get imaginative with colour changes in your flooring to create zones – you could even use several tints of the same hue to make a gentler, gradient-style transition.

DIY basics

working with wood

Being able to carry out basic DIY is both empowering and cost-saving, allowing you to create exactly what you want for your space (and giving you a sense of pride once you've finished it, too). Once you've mastered a few basic rules and techniques, you might want to try taking things further and create your own bespoke pieces.

While there are, of course, many instances where professional help is necessary, before automatically booking in a tradesperson consider if this is something you could tackle either solo or collaboratively instead: for example, having wood cut to size, or having built-in furniture fitted for you, but then finishing it off yourself.

tips from the trade:
some insider insights

By Steve Wilson, Master Carpenter for Interior Design Masters

As a general rule I'd call in the trades if you're not sure on anything, even if only for advice, which most builders will give free of charge. Go with a personal recommendation where possible – anyone can say they know what they are doing but try to get someone who has proven they can do it.

+ If you're totally renovating a room at home, consider the order for works during first fix and second fix, versus what to leave until the end.

+ Adding in any new structures or built-in furniture? There's no point wasting time getting walls or surfaces looking good if you're going to hide them, so plan in advance.

+ When stripping walls or preparing walls and woodwork for painting, as the saying goes, 'fail to prepare, then prepare to fail'. Time spent prepping, sanding and filling walls and woodwork will pay back dividends in the finished results.

Which wood?

Your choice of construction material can come down to both personal preferences and practical functionality, but these are the most commonly used for building and boxing-in:

- **Pine:** an inexpensive softwood, pine is easy to work with and a good option for projects where you'd still like to be able to see the grain.
- **MDF:** an engineered composite, MDF is cheap and smooth, making it a popular choice for a range of applications. However, it can lack strength, plus it contains chemical compounds that can be harmful to inhale when cutting it. As well as solid sheets, you can also get flexible ribbed MDF; the ribs enable it to curve and are intended to be hidden, but if you want a slatted look use them on the outside instead.
- **Plywood:** created from cross-laminated thin sheets, plywood is strong yet lightweight, and has an inherent natural flex, making it good for curved applications. Its pleasing looks come at a premium though, and it's not the easiest material to cut.
- **OSB:** short for Oriented Strand Board, this manufactured board is inexpensive and contains a consistent density, making it a popular choice for flat applications like sub-flooring. Its industrial look has seen it grow in popularity for more visible applications, but it can swell if it gets damp and is therefore best avoided in kitchens and bathrooms.

'In my own kitchen at home, I had an ugly gas meter cupboard I wanted to hide, so I made a bespoke floor-to-ceiling cupboard from moisture-resistant MDF. I measured up to work out the sizes I'd need for the side panels and door, then purchased this from a DIY store which offered a free cutting service, so it was just a case then of screwing it all together rather than needing to hire a tradesman to build me something bespoke... it's easier than you think to do it yourself.'

Rochelle Dalphinis, Design Contestant, Series 3

fixtures
and fittings

Sockets, switches, hooks, handles, radiators and any other fitted elements in the home are important to consider within an overall scheme – often the basic models can be exactly that, and could throw off the whole look (think a bog-standard white radiator in an otherwise completely dark and moody decorative scheme).

While there are plenty of companies willing to sell you designer radiators and statement switches, these costs can quickly add up – especially if you're overhauling your entire house. But get creative and you can save cash as well as create a bespoke finish:

Radiators

- Paint a basic radiator the same colour as the wall it's on to visually erase it. Making sure it's switched off, sand and clean it first before preparing it with a radiator primer, then paint it with the same emulsion you used on your walls (cheaper paints might flake over time due to the heat: if you're concerned, finish it with a radiator sealer).
- Want a statement look? Use radiator-friendly spray paint, allowing you to go for bolder finishes such as neons or metallics. Prep as above, making sure to protect all surrounding walls and surfaces.
- Alternatively, cover it. Search online for sleek clip-on fitted covers and magnetic radiator 'wraps', which simply magnetise to the front. Or, to turn it into a storage area, add a radiator cover with an integrated slim shelf top.

Light switches and plug sockets

- Plastic switch plates can be painted or sprayed, too, using the same method as left, though obviously anything electrical needs to be approached carefully. Switch off the power supply before removing the switch plates, then work on them elsewhere before reattaching. Several thin, light coats will work best.
- Want to inject some pattern? Remove your switch plates as above, but cover them with some extra-wide decorative washi (a Japanese masking tape), instead. Use a scalpel to carefully cut around toggle switches or plug pin holes.

'To bring a sense of unity into my own small home, I opted for brass as my material of choice across all my fixtures and fittings. Having this common thread allows you to be bolder in other areas – without one uniting element things can look clumsy, but taking this approach across a whole house helps bring everything together.'

Temi Johnson, Design Contestant, Series 4

handle and hook alternatives

While existing metal handles and hooks can also be transformed with a coat of spray paint, thinking outside the box could yield even more imaginative solutions.

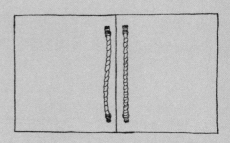

Hooks

+ Vintage walking sticks can be re-imagined as hooks, as they were in Banjo's 'drunk botanist' bedroom in Series 3, episode 2 (above). Saw off some of their length if needed, then screw directly through them to fix in place on the wall (or use a saddle clip to secure them).

+ Fix some pretty drawer pulls onto a wooden batten, then screw the batten directly into your wall for an alternative hook set.

+ Ditch the DIY and fix some wooden clothes pegs to your walls as hooks, using Velcro pads to secure them.

Handles

+ Create some rustic rope handles to soften a shiny kitchen, like Paul did in Series 3, episode 7 (above). Cut your ropes to length, then burn the ends with a lighter to seal the fibres. Thread a screw directly through both the rope and the existing handle holes, and fix on the inside of your cupboard door. If you're concerned about grubby marks, slip a leather cuff over the centre of the rope before attaching it.

+ Wrapping existing bar handles in twine gives a similar look for a lot less DIY. Fix the start and end of the twine using a hot glue gun.

+ Glue some oversized buttons onto flat-fronted circular handles for some vintage charm.

working with wall tiles

Often confined to kitchens and bathrooms, wall tiles can also bring both practicality and a wow factor to most other rooms in the home if you think outside the box a little.

Ways to lay

You needn't necessarily spend a fortune on designer tiles – by playing with different configurations and elevating your grouting, you can create a more luxe end result with even a basic tile.

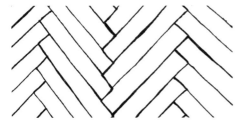

Herringbone

Offers a chic twist on the more classic brick bond layout. A diagonal herringbone arrangement encourages your eye to move around the space more.

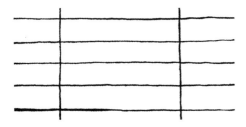

Stack bond

Create a contemporary, graphic look by laying rectangular tiles horizontally or vertically rather than in the more standard staggered brick formation.

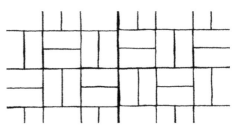

Basketweave

Placing pairs of tiles together to create almost geometric-style shapes looks striking (but can also take longer to lay).

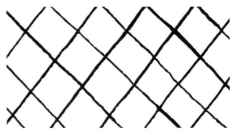

Diamond

Arranging square tiles on their sides works well for chequerboard colour choices, and helps blur the boundaries of the space (which is beneficial in smaller spots).

How to tile

While it's not an intrinsically difficult job, if you've never tiled before watch some online demonstration videos before you try it out. But in essence, you will need to use a trowel to spread tile adhesive over sections

tip

Many retailers offer tiles in a range of colours and finishes within the same product line. Try mixing and matching for a more organic look, as used by Lynsey in her beach hut in Series 2, episode 5, where she mixed simple white metro tiles with pastel-toned and textured ones from the same range, adding in the odd mirror tile to reflect the coastline opposite.

where else to use?

Love the look of tiles? Try using them in other areas of the home:

+   To create an alternative headboard by tiling behind your bedhead area.

+   Along the lower third of a busy, narrow hallway (it'll add interest and protect against scuffs).

+   Across any rendered outside walls, for a Mediterranean look (make sure any tiles you choose are appropriate for exterior use).

of your wall before laying each tile before it dries, using tile spacers as you go. You'll likely need a tile cutter (or a tile scribe knife and metal ruler) to cut tiles to size so they fit into corners or around any pipes. Once dry, you'll be able to move on to grouting. Different walls will require different prep, but you can also tile directly on top of an old set of tiles to minimise the disruption.

Get playful with grout

-   Grout comes in a surprising range of colours to either co-ordinate or contrast with your chosen tiles (if you go to a specialist tile shop, they should be able to show you samples). Bold coloured grout can be a great middle-ground option if you're keen for a more unusual look, but are anxious about going for bold tile

designs (far easier to re-grout than re-tile if you change your mind).

-   For existing tiles where the grouting is fundamentally sound, try a grout pen for an instant, easy refresh. White will freshen things up, or, to create a more contemporary graphic look, opt for a grey or black, which instantly transforms basic white square tiles into something geometric and considered.

-   Want a gilded look? Try adding some Mapei Mapeglitter (a coloured metallic glitter designed to be mixed with epoxy resin grout), or you could experiment with adding a fine glitter powder like mica into grout. Always follow the manufacturer's instructions for the correct ratios (or do a patch test if you're trying your own bespoke blend).

See pages 210–211 for examples of tiles used in creative decorating projects.

Essential components

Fireplaces

If you're in a period property, hopefully you've been lucky enough to inherit an original fireplace on any chimney breasts. While in decades past it became fashionable to remove ornate mantlepieces (or even knock out the chimney breast altogether), in recent years they have become a far more celebrated feature, giving both structure and character to a room.

It can prove challenging, however, if you've inherited a boxed-in flat wall, or an empty hole where a hearth would once have sat. Here's how you can turn them back into more of a focal point:

- If there's space, introduce an electric stove which mimics the look of a wood burner (either standing it in the hole, or in front of the boarded-up area); powered by electricity, they don't need the installation that the real thing requires.
- Turn a hole into more of a feature by placing a mantel beam across the top, providing display space. A 'floating' style, which attaches to the wall via keyhole fixings on the back, gives a seamless look. Fill the hole itself with decorative logs and string lights, or get creative and add in some shelves and a cushion to turn it into a tiny reading nook, or make it into a plant corner.
- If the entire chimney breast has been removed and you're left with a totally flat wall, place a slim cabinet or console table where the hearth and mantel would have been to give it a new focal point.

The elephant in the room

It's more sympathetic design-wise to avoid having your TV competing with your fireplace for dominance, so place it off-centre in either alcove, or on a different wall altogether, if you can. If there's no other space for it to go, see if you can switch your basic black screen for a 'frame' TV (which displays a choice of art prints on its screen when not in use), or work out a clever way to disguise it (see pages 226–227 for ideas on hiding your tech).

tip

Inherited an ornate fireplace but minimal is more your style? Don't rip it out: embrace the juxtaposition, or paint it the same colour as your walls to visually tone it down.

DEAN'S DARK-AND-MOODY BEDROOM

A boarded-up fireplace can still be beautiful, as seen in Dean's hotel bedroom design in Series 3, episode 2. Decorative wood trim has been used across the boarded area to nod to the style of the mantlepiece, and, by painting both elements the same colour, the boarded section isn't highlighted and so blends in. The added bonus of the black background also helps the TV blend in with the equally dark walls.

'For me, the use of black in this room has paid off: it's very eccentric and bold. I think I've hit the nail on the head here with the brief of 'British eccentric', because it's truly British to be a little different.'

Dean Powell, Design Contestant, Series 3

The lowdown on paint

Paint offers one of the most powerful ways to completely change the look of your room with relatively little outlay and skill requirements. But with so many different products and brands on the market, it can be a minefield figuring out what to use where. Here's what you need to know:

Product types and finishes

Primers and undercoats:

Broadly speaking, any bare surface will need priming to prepare it for a coat of paint (especially if it's a shiny or difficult surface like melamine or metal). Sealers and undercoats (the term is sometimes interchangeable) are normally only required if the surface being painted has an unstable finish, such as previously water-damaged walls, or if switching from a dark to light topcoat. Previously painted surfaces in sound condition should be good to go – just give them a clean first.

Sheen:

Different brands will have slightly different names for their finishes, but flat and matte paints will contain a very low level of sheen, with the scale working upwards towards satin, soft sheen and mid sheen. Wood paints generally aren't flat matte (as this isn't very hardwearing), so tend to start with eggshell, which has a subtle sheen, going up to full gloss. Lower-sheen paints can be more forgiving and subtle, making them a good choice for older properties with imperfect surfaces. Mid-sheen and gloss finishes are more hardwearing, but can also show up any lumps and bumps. For a subtle effect, use different sheens on different surfaces in the same room.

Make-up:

Some paints can contain VOCs (volatile organic compounds), which can be toxic and strong-smelling. Increasingly, modern paint brands are minimising or completely removing their VOC content, which is

tip

Always keep a note - digitally or in a dedicated notebook - of exactly what paint you've used where, and in what finish. If you've got leftover paint at the end of a job, transfer it to a glass jar and label it with both the colour and where you've used it, to prevent it drying out (or forgetting where it's from).

especially beneficial if you have young children around. Water-based gloss paints have almost completely taken over from oil-based gloss, and as well as being far kinder to the environment, they are also much easier to work with.

Specialist paints

Chalk paint:

More commonly used for furniture, it has (unsurprisingly) a chalky matte consistency, yet is thick and hardwearing. It's usually applied directly onto surfaces without priming or sanding, but can require a coat of wax at the end instead, and is often used to create aged paint effects.

Spray paint:

With a wide range of colours, spray paints are generally a versatile product suitable for all sorts of applications, but for any larger-scale surfaces (or to ensure you are colour matching), use an electric paint sprayer you can fill with standard emulsion.

Limewash:

A traditional, natural paint that is especially good for old walls which need to breathe (modern emulsions can cause them problems), but it's also a good option for a characterful, period look in a newer home.

Room-specific:

Many paint manufacturers offer specialist paint for heavy-duty spaces like kitchens, bathrooms and hallways, designed to be more wipe-clean and water resistant.

Mixing your own colour:

If you're struggling to find the perfect shade, or are trying to remedy a paint you've already purchased, remember the rules regarding tones and tints: adding in white will simply make a paler version, whereas adding grey or black will make it more muted and earthy (and darker). Combine paints with the same sheen and remember, if you run out of your bespoke mix, it'll be near-impossible to recreate.

'I love to use the same paint colour in two different finishes to create a modern chair rail effect (where the paint treatment is different on the lower third of the wall), with a matte finish paint on the top two thirds and a satin finish below. It looks great in hallways, especially if you take the line a little higher to chest height.'

Tom Power, Design Contestant, Series 4

wallpaper 101

Wallpaper has swung firmly back into fashion after a period of pattern-free minimalism, and new paste-the-wall technologies make it far easier to use than traditional paste-the-paper types.

Using wallpaper creatively can be a great way to reflect your signature style. You might want to try wrapping a textural pattern round two adjoining walls to create a cocooning corner, or even across a whole room for an immersive, boundary-blurring feel. Printing technology has allowed murals to become more cost-effective, too: although often more expensive than standard papers, the results can be show-stopping and you could balance the cost by skipping additional wall art.

Consider your surrounding colours carefully: it's far easier to find paint colours to complement, contrast or match your chosen wallpaper design than to find a paper to match your paint. Pull out a hue or two from its overall pattern design: for a calming, tonal look, keep it similar to the dominant backing colour or, for a quirkier scheme, pull out accents from less obvious details within its pattern.

Different paper types

- Textured and embossed: papers like Anaglypta and Lincrusta are a great option for bringing in period charm and subtle texture, and can be painted to your preference. 'Textured' can also refer to flocked and damask patterns,

plus naturally textured finishes such as grasscloth.
- Vinyl: composed of a coated layer over a printed design, this hardwearing paper is great for durability (especially in steamy or humid rooms), but its finish can look a little synthetic.
- Non-woven: a breathable product, non-woven paper comprises both synthetic and natural fibres, resulting in a strong paper that's generally easier to apply and remove than its vinyl counterparts (and it tends to look more natural, too).
- Peel-and-stick: great for renters, this ready-to go paper is removable but can be tricky to hang and is usually more expensive than standard papers.

Order of works

Whether you're painting, papering, or doing both, here's what you'll need, and the workflow to follow (as you may have guessed, it's best to start with paint!):

- Prep your space: lay down dust sheets, turn off the power supply and unscrew electrical face plates and light fittings. Fill/sand/clean all surfaces as appropriate.
- Starting at the ceiling, begin 'cutting in'

tips from the trade:
pro decorating hacks

By Jo Pollock, business owner at Ladies Who Paint and set decorator for Interior Design Masters

+   Always follow the steps listed on your paint tin/the side of your wallpaper's packaging - as application methods do vary between products and brands.

+   As they say, buy cheap pay twice: whether it's cheap paint, brushes or rollers, you'll get a better finish if you buy trade-quality products and won't need as much, either.

+   Use plastic bags or bin liners to line your paint scuttle - it saves on both washing up and paint wastage. Also keep extra bags or cling film on hand to protect brushes and rollers from drying out between applications.

+   It's ALL about the preparation as well as the application. When painting, avoid stopping mid area as it creates a block shade - always keep a wet edge until you finish that area, or stop at your room's corners if you can't finish the whole room.

(using a brush to paint a band along the edge where the ceiling meets the wall). Work in sections then – before the paint dries – fill in the surrounding portion of ceiling using a short–pile 9-inch roller. Move down to the walls, cutting in around the edges again as you go.

-   Move on to woodwork (if you want to continue with the exact same colour, use a colour-matched wood paint – your wall emulsion won't adhere well). For more ornate architrave, you may need a smaller brush to get into any nooks and crannies as well as a larger one for flat surfaces.

-   Applying your wallpaper depends on its type so always follow the manufacturer's instructions. If you haven't papered before, buy a full wallpaper hanging kit, for everything you'll need. If you're short on space, opt for paste-the-wall, which allows you to forego a pasting table and allows more time for repositioning before it dries.

'Certain suppliers will only send you a small wallpaper sample if you order online so see if you can visit a showroom to see a larger sample in situ, especially if the pattern is quite large. Some DIY stores allow you to tear off the amount you like from sample rolls (save the offcuts for any small upcycling projects, to minimise waste).'

Edward Robinson, Design Producer, Interior Design Masters

For some more creative wallpaper application ideas, see pages 208–209.

Essential components

Fabric and pattern

Turning to fabric and pattern is one of the easiest ways to create an interesting, tactile and cohesive design scheme. Design is, of course, subjective, so while declaring certain pattern, fabric or colour combinations as 'right' or 'wrong' can feel reductive, it's worth creating your framework based on your aesthetic goals and signature style.

Which fabrics?

Pattern or plain, your choice of fabrics plays a part in your design story, and introducing several different types of material can help create depth and interest. Here's what's most commonly used in interiors:

- For creating texture: fabrics with a looser weave and heavier thread count can help create a more tactile feel; think muslin and voile for lightweight, semi-sheer applications. For a more rustic look, hessian and even coffee sacking can bring a pastoral aesthetic, though these are best

how to: paint upholstered furniture

By Amy Wilson, Design Contestant, Series 2

Did you know you can paint fabric? Design contestant Amy shared the technique in episode 2, by painting existing upholstered armchairs (shown right) to create something more visually interesting.

+ First, clean your furniture and test your paint on an inconspicuous section before going all in (generally speaking, plain cotton or polycotton pieces without much pile will work best). If you're creating a band of colour or want to avoid painting certain details, apply masking tape where required. Use a spray bottle filled with water to dampen your furniture, then brush or sponge on a diluted layer of emulsion paint (play with the ratios - you'll likely find half-and-half, or two-thirds paint to one-third water, works best). Once dry, sand with very fine sandpaper (which will prevent the finished piece feeling crispy or the paint flaking off), then repeat the process until you're happy with the end result.

+ This technique can also work well on furniture with intricate detailing, such as button-back chairs, which would be harder to reupholster than a more basic boxy design.

used at windows as they can be a little scratchy on the skin. Bouclé and shearling used on sofas and armchairs can feel like you're sitting in a cloud.

- For casual sophistication: with its gently crumpled looks, linen only gets better with age. While not the cheapest choice, it's a wise investment, and brings with it an air of laid-back sophistication. Slub silk, with its irregular texture, has a similar aesthetic but has a little more sheen to it, making it a good option for gloomier spaces thanks to its light-bouncing qualities.

- For durability: furniture upholstery requires sturdy, hardwearing fabrics which can ideally be washed (or steam/spot cleaned). Ticking, canvas and brushed cotton work well for upholstered seating

or, for a luxe look, leather (or vinyl) and velvet will do the job (though stick to polyester velvet if spills and stains might be an issue).

When choosing any fabric, it's important to keep its end-use in mind. If, for example, you've fallen in love with a print that's on a lightweight cotton, it probably won't be durable enough to work as sofa upholstery but perhaps it'd be OK to cover a seat pad on an occasional chair. It's also important to factor in sustainability, too: where possible, recycled or organic natural materials can offer the smallest carbon footprint, though increasingly there are interesting, sustainable synthetic alternatives such as Tencel and Piñatex.

playing with pattern

Different designs

- Traditional patterns like Toile de Jouy bring a faded grandeur to both sophisticated and more rustic settings.
- Spots, stripes and checks can almost be considered a 'non-pattern', and are easier to blend with other more intricate designs for a layered look.
- Floral designs range from the small and ditsy to big, blousy watercolour styles. If in doubt when mixing them, stick to designs that share a similar language (this could be a colour palette, or opting for only abstract floral patterns rather than mixing them with more realistic interpretations).
- If you're wary of going too busy, choose simpler patterns for items like curtains and sofas, then have fun with bolder, more playful elements in removable accents like cushions and tablecloths. Details like a contrasting box pleat within a valance, or the piping trim on a cushion, can also offer a subtle way to add more pattern or tie a scheme together (and are a great way to use up any scraps and offcuts).

how to: design your own print pattern

By Amy Davies, Design Contestant, Series 3

Producing designs professionally can be a lengthy, detailed process that involves professional software, but there's nothing to stop you adapting the process to create your own designs at home. Creating a print for fabric or as an artwork can be a fun way of seeing your creations come to life.

Start with your artwork - use any medium you like to create it, be that pencil, watercolours, pastels, chalks, acrylic paint or collage. Once you have your artwork ready, scan it into your computer, then save the design as a JPG file. If you want to edit or manipulate the design to create a repeat pattern you may need to use an editing software like Adobe Photoshop, though for simpler tweaks your existing scanner or photo-editing software may suffice.

Search online for a fabric-specialist printer (their website may also feature software where you can create a repeat pattern as part of the ordering process); most will be glad to help guide you and advise on the best fabrics to print on in order to achieve your vision.

advice from the experts:
ways to work with pattern and texture

By Kit Kemp, Interior Designer and Guest Judge

+   I love using bold patterns in my work, from traditional florals to smart stripes and modern, graphic designs - especially motif-heavy repeats that tell a story. These designs are often the hardest to use: you have to be brave and bold when working with busy patterns, but also know when to pare it back.

+   To me, the best interiors marry different textures and unexpected details within the scheme. When choosing textures and colour palettes, I always consider the natural light within a room first: if it is a cold, indirect light, layers of textures, felt embroidery and patterned fabrics make a room feel warm. In a sunny room with good light, a darker colour on the walls works well, contrasted with brighter fabrics on the upholstery. Without texture interiors can look flat and cold, so layering rough and smooth, cosy with sleek, and embellished or carved with clean and plain is one of the most important parts of my design process. This tactility and attention to detail captures, satisfies and inspires all of the senses.

+   I gravitate towards fabrics that are rich with natural imperfections and texture within the weave - it's an easy and immediate way to imbue a space with understated luxury. A blend of linens, wools, weaves and prints lends depth to a room, as raised surfaces reflect light and create shadows.

+   Covering walls with fabric has become one of my hallmarks. I like using linen because it is at once comfortable yet effortlessly chic. It's cocooning, absorbing sound and adding warmth, yet tailored and hard-wearing.

'It's important to play around with the scale and type of the pattern you're using (for example, mixing stripes with animal print, or gingham with ditsy florals) whilst always being mindful that the tones of the different colours work in harmony.'

Joanne Hardcastle, Design Contestant, Series 4

JU'S PORTUGUESE-INSPIRED BEDROOM

Known for her bright, colourful style and use of both bold patterns and floral prints, Ju designed this hotel bedroom (Series 1, episode 2) to feel light and sophisticated but also playful, aiming to give visitors a joyful experience. Blending several different patterns in the room, she showed how pattern mixing doesn't necessarily result in a busy or heavy-looking design.

The space

Ju wanted to nod to the seaside location of this space (on the English coast) but in a less obvious way, so she introduced a Portuguese twist to bring in the 'holiday feels', picking a bold tile-effect wallpaper and colours that evoked the mood of the Mediterranean. She also referenced the Victorian heritage of the building through period-appropriate accents, like the oriental rug and decorative urn-style plant pot.

Get the look

+ Ju's bedroom space mixed no fewer than four different patterns, but to ensure they all worked together she kept to a consistent colour palette of blues and whites, with fresh spring-inspired greens, mauves and yellows as accents.

+ To stop a multi-patterned space feeling chaotic, use bold block colours to break things up (as seen here with the headboard and curtains). This also helps ensure any contrasting patterns (on both the wall and bed, here) don't directly meet. A striped black and white trim on the cushions adds a subtle touch of modernity.

+ Think outside the box: to continue her al fresco feel, Ju used exterior wall lanterns in place of standard bedside wall lights. Generally speaking, outdoor electric wall lights should work in exactly the same way as their interiors counterparts, and can be hard-wired into your wall as normal, but check with an electrician before purchasing a pair to ensure the voltage is appropriate. You'll also need to consider functionality - ideally, install each with its own independent light switch on either side of the bed, rather than having to turn them on and off via your main light switch.

'I wanted to create a space that people would feel good in, and provide a sense of escapism. I like to create spaces that are unique, break the boundaries, and most importantly put a smile on people's faces when they walk in ... that's always my end goal! This concept was a risky move, as my designs are definitely not everyone's cup of tea, but this task was all about showing my signature style, so I'm glad I went for it!'

Ju De Paula, Design Contestant, Series 1

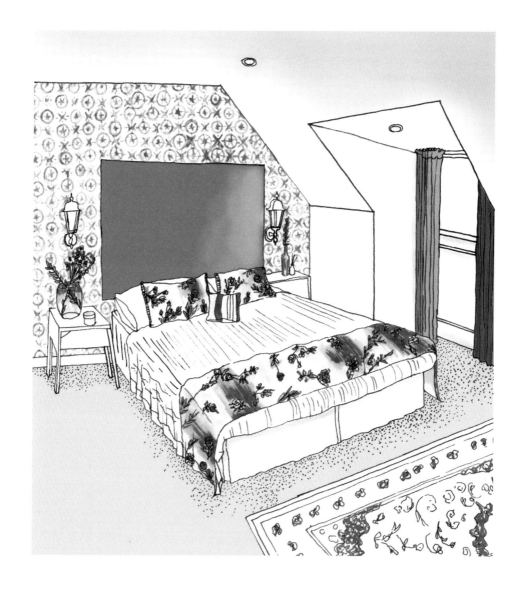

5

Design styles and signature styles

'I like helping the true architectural character of original buildings to shine, using (or restoring) existing features where possible and contrasting them with modern treatments. I'm wary of producing a replica, though, and prefer to create a space with a subtle nod to the past, which can be juxtaposed with vintage and contemporary elements for a truly unique space.'

Linda Boronkay, Interior Designer and Guest Judge

Decor by period

Georgian, Victorian and Edwardian style

While you needn't let specific aspects – such as age, style or budget – dictate your overall approach wholeheartedly, it's nonetheless important to consider these together and work with rather than against them. By getting to know the bones of your home a little better, and familiarising yourself with its key features (and flaws), you can create a look that plays to its strengths but is also inherently 'you'. Here's some guidance on the most common house styles in the UK, and how you might make their key features work for you (or borrow them, if your home is from a different era).

Georgian (1714–1810)

Style and features

Inspired by the 16th-century Italian Renaissance, typical Georgian homes favoured symmetry, relying on generous and well-balanced proportions, such as large windows and high ceilings, to add a refined elegance. Letting the building itself do the talking, Georgian interiors typically didn't feature lavish decorations, and incorporated symmetrical room layouts and stylish details like fanlight windows above doorways, crown mouldings and ceiling roses to embellish them.

Get the look

Work with the symmetry these spaces offer by balancing furniture or fitted details such as alcove shelving (or create this in your own space by setting a focal point then working symmetrically either side of it). The Georgians were big fans of column details, influenced by Ancient Greece; bringing through fluted accents and details will nod to this. Greyed-off mid-tones like pea green and burgundy looked elegant in these well-lit rooms, though the later Georgian era saw the popularity for pastels rise, too: mauves and – of course – Regency Blue typify the palette.

Victorian (1839–1900)

Style and features

Victorian homes were often hurriedly thrown up to meet the ever-growing housing needs created by the Industrial Revolution, and range from modest 'two-up, two-down' terraced houses designed for low-paid workers to grander neo-Gothic-inspired showpieces for the wealthy. Designs were often asymmetric (partly due to necessity, to cram in as much accommodation as possible). Despite their fussiness and flaws (often featuring perpetually dark middle rooms and a narrow footprint), their generous ceiling heights and charming period details, from sash windows and wrought iron fireplaces to cornicing and carved architraves, mean they're still top of many house buyers' wishlist; and despite the hasty construction, they are surprisingly sturdy.

Get the look

With their lack of plumbing and electricity, Victorian homes were hard to keep clean so were decorated in deep, rich tones like burgundy and dark green, and their high ceilings, generous windows and smaller footprints mean today's Victorian homes work just as well with this darker palette. The Victorian predilection for 'busy' interiors, filled with trinkets and art, might not be everyone's cup of tea, but they certainly weren't boring!

Edwardian (1900–1918)

Style and features

A little more subdued than the height of the Victorian era, Edwardian properties tend to be more evenly balanced, with slightly lower ceilings made up for by their wider footprints. In line with the Arts and Crafts movement, which favoured a humbler approach that respected nature, homes were more likely to feature simpler timber details and timeless tiles. With electricity becoming more commonplace, wall lights and lamps became highly fashionable, alongside higher contrast surfaces like glossy block flooring and dark lacquered wood furniture.

Get the look

Prints and patterns influenced by the earlier work of William Morris suit Edwardian spaces (and bring a simplistic charm to homes from other eras, too), as do warm, earthy tones. The influence of Art Nouveau later led to pastel tones returning to popularity, which sit sympathetically against the glossy dark floors and furniture.

'Because Victorian style is so rich and sumptuous, I like to approach it in a maximalist way. To create a moody and romantic Victorian vibe, I tend to have lots of lamps scattered around the space and I always choose warm, vintage-style Edison style light bulbs.'

Monika Charchula, Design Contestant, Series 4

Art Deco and Mid-century style

Art Deco (1920–1940)

Style and features

Heavily influenced by Ancient Egypt (Tutankhamun's tomb was discovered in 1922, drawing huge interest to this style), and buoyed by a spirit of post-war exuberance, Art Deco can be characterised by its simple, geometric shapes and rich, opulent colours. It was all about looking forward, which architects achieved by embracing new materials and technologies to produce a very different style of housing to previous generations.

Interiors favoured a more open layout than the tiny warren of rooms in many Victorian homes, and design details were streamlined, both as a result of the freedom that building with steel and concrete provided and as cinema gave us a window into the architectural styles being used in other countries.

Borrowing from Deco style, albeit in a more conservative manner, the classic 1930s semi began to spring up across the burgeoning new suburban towns that were hastily being created after the war. With space to spread out, these properties were far more generously proportioned than the typical Victorian terraces of the cities.

Get the look

Deco-influenced designs continue to remain popular to this day, with the style regularly trending. Borrow influences without slavishly reproducing it by keeping in mind where your own style begins: do you love the gold accents and bold, geometric patterns, or would the period's classic curved furniture and sleek accent pieces suit you better?

Mid-century Modern (1945–1969)

Style and features

With roots in the USA (where it was in turn influenced by Germany's Bauhaus movement a couple of decades earlier), the Modernist movement showcased a radical lack of ornamentation and a preference for design harmony, favouring functionality over fussy design details which might unnecessarily clutter the space. Houses, and the items within them, were designed to be multi-use, geometric and streamlined, featuring fully open-plan layouts and glazed facades which facilitated a greater connection between inside and out.

Many designers took a joined-up approach, with classic furniture from the era designed to fit perfectly with this broader design ethos. This level of consideration resulted in highly desirable and covetable pieces which look just as cutting-edge today and continue to appear in fashionable homes, such as the Eames lounger and Ercol Windsor dining chair.

Get the look

Mid-century style somehow manages to look achingly modern and on-trend to this day, despite its roots going back almost a century. While distinctive in appearance, with its clean lines and geometric shapes, furniture from this era blends almost effortlessly into most interiors, bringing a contemporary juxtaposition to period properties or delivering a slice of vintage cool to new-build spaces.

'The best Mid-century pieces can usually be found at your local thrift shop, boot sale or flea market. When choosing, focus on shape over finish: Mid-century furniture is often made from long-lasting hard wood species like oak, walnut and teak (anything made from these would cost a pretty penny today).'

Karl Mok, Design Contestant, Series 4

'A lot of people think that Art Deco style is always really pared back and simple, and although in some cases that's true, it was also a time of flamboyance and decadence. Animal prints were a big thing during this time, along with lots of colour and pattern.

I live in a beautiful Art Deco house filled with lots of original features which I wanted to enhance and preserve, but I didn't want to create a time capsule or museum-like home. So I have taken some elements of Art Deco but given it a modern-day twist. My house is full of beautiful animal prints, feathered lamps, velvet cocktail chairs, gold leaf ceilings and wall-to-wall murals: it's flamboyant, and gives a modern take on Deco with a glamorous edge.'

Siobhan Murphy, Design Contestant, Series 2

Design styles and signature styles

Retro and modern-day homes

Retro homes (1970s)

Style and features

With the post-war babies now setting up their own adult homes, and the design influence of the 1960s Space Age still going strong, modern young couples were keen to move away from the fussier spaces and design styles of their childhoods and into these contemporary new homes with their large, flat windows and open plan layouts. With central heating now widespread, fireplaces were no longer needed, resulting in flat walls and far simpler architectural features (either a good or bad thing, depending on your personal preference).

Design-wise, the 1970s are (somewhat unfairly) widely thought of as 'the decade that taste forgot', referring to key design moments such as the avocado bathroom suite, shag-pile carpets and lurid psychedelic patterns. Typical colours of the era were equally divisive, with its key palette of browns and oranges punctuated with vibrant reds and turquoise. Yet many of these details are quietly sneaking their way back into fashion, with coloured bathroom suites beginning to re-emerge in modern showrooms and the joy of long-piled carpets and rugs being rediscovered for their luxe looks and under-foot comfort.

Get the look

Arguably one of the most 'Marmite' of all the design periods, retro style tends to be something you either love or hate. But it's a surprisingly easy look to mix in with other styles (and eras), too, especially off-shoot trends such as earthy boho schemes incorporating the classic rattan peacock chair and other natural materials. Even the houseplants popular in the '70s are enjoying a resurgence, as we rush to fill our homes with nostalgic spider and cheese plants. Teak furniture, with its warm orange undertone, remains easy to live with, offering a lighter look than the typical darker browns of earlier period pieces.

Modern-day houses and apartments

Style and features

While the 1980s and '90s typically favoured postmodern, traditionally inspired housing, borrowing many design features from the Victorian and inter-war eras (often accused of appearing pastiche), the 2000s onwards have swung back into a more neomodern, minimalist direction. With many of us continuing to flock to cities, space is at a premium, and as a result the move to convert many now-redundant industrial buildings has influenced the style of new-build homes and apartments, too. Industrial elements offer the aspects of character and authenticity that were somewhat lost once traditional fireplaces and cornicing became redundant: now we crave exposed steel joists, bare brickwork and factory-style Crittall-look windows, instead.

Get the look

Modern homes are often criticised for a lack of space or ill-thought-out footprints, designed to squeeze in as many housing units as possible with little consideration for the liveability of those residing in them. But on the plus side, they offer a blank canvas to imbue with aspects from many other design eras. Consider building in fitted furniture, adding panelled wall detailing or creating your own focal points and layout structures, blending together the designs and styles you naturally favour. Modernist elements, with their clean lines, can work well here, playing upon the simplicity (and any industrial details) in a new space. If yours comes with any obviously faux accents, such as a modern mantlepiece screwed into a flat wall, consider losing it altogether, or make it look a little more convincing by building out a faux chimney breast to turn it into more of an authentic focal point.

Often, it's the dearth of authentic materials in new-build spaces that can lead to a lack of character: try painting uPVC windows or mock-wood fire doors in dark metal tones, switch out cheap-looking hardware and handles, and throw down some textural vintage rugs over any laminate wood floors.

'The basement bar I redesigned (in episode 8 - illustrated on page 76) offered a little unexpected treasure trove of all things 70s. An ode to the era, I included textured fabrics, geometric patterned wallpaper, bold burnt orange tones, iconic furniture and even shag-pile carpet (all while trying not to be too cliché).

The thing I love about that decade's decor is that it has held its place in history, as well as offering a rich reference point for modern interiors. It's the era that keeps giving, constantly lending its brilliant forms, patterns, scales and details to new modern and contemporary styles.'

Amy Davies, Design Contestant, Series 3

combining different periods

While mixing up your design metaphors can lead to a look that feels confusing, there are elements of similarity to be found in pieces from all eras – the trick is working out what unites them all so you can successfully mix aspects of different eras together to fit your signature style.

Consider ways you can blend different eras together, such as painting vintage furniture in a contemporary colourway (or part-painting pieces, to juxtapose the original wood against a modern hue). Equally, you can add character to modern melamine furniture using chalk paint, which provides a textural, gently aged look. Many retro furniture pieces share a similarity with more streamlined Mid-century designs, for example, or introduce industrial-style pieces into a Victorian home: while they may not have originally been there, they could be from the same design era.

'Each project I work on centres on how people live and inhabit a space, and my approach to design tries to focus on the experience and the atmosphere the client is aiming to create. I always carry out detailed research into each project: with a new-build, I will research the history of the area, and work with local craftspeople to produce pieces that add character and have meaning. Artworks are important as they can change the tempo of a room. I like to use vintage pieces that bring character and narrative, as well as layers of colour and texture through the soft furnishings.'

Linda Boronkay, *Interior Designer and Guest Judge*

'Mixing in period furniture gives instant character and personality you can't get from buying new. For example, a beaten-up chunky antique dresser with layers of age from a previous life adds more interest and depth than something shiny and new (though a mix of both is an absolute look!). I think a modern interior calls for predominantly modern additions BUT adding the odd statement piece from the Georgian, Victorian or even Art Deco era gives instant interest, a bit like a museum or gallery... it's a showpiece.'

Jack Kinsey, *Design Contestant, Series 4*

advice from the experts:
how to mix modernity with period style

By Guy Oliver, Principal Designer/Owner at Oliver Laws Ltd and Guest Judge

The secret to designing a successful scheme in a heritage building is not to slavishly reproduce a period – unless that was the brief. These spaces aren't museums, they are people's homes and have to function as such in the contemporary world. People buy period properties because they like their character, or they feel they are more substantially built than modern buildings. But equally, they need to integrate modern technology and services.

It's important to respect and be sensitive to these historic elements by restoring or repairing the fabric of a room or building, discreetly introducing heating and lighting then layering in items that reflect the owner's character and personality. Making a historic interior feel contemporary can be achieved through the use of block colour, how the space is lit, and the use of art and objects. A good designer will weave a story through the prism of their experience and the result should be a convincing whole.

There's a long-running argument about authenticity and taste: just because something is old, it doesn't mean that it is appropriate, and just because it is the latest fashion, it doesn't mean that it is tried and tested and will work in a period property.

A space should be intuitively designed and create the desired atmosphere. Everyone's taste is different and there is no right and wrong, but there is experience, and that is where the designer comes in. I worked with one client who had their 18th-century property decorated by a museum consultant, but then they found they couldn't use the rooms because the furniture was laid out in a style typical of that period (around the perimeter of the rooms). This left no room for the elements of real life, like a TV or comfortable furniture, so the family ended up spending most of their time in the basement. They called me in to undo what had been done and to make it liveable, which I achieved by mixing and layering the antique objects with comfortable (and appropriate) sofas and chairs, so their house became a home.

Design styles and signature styles

projects with a period nod

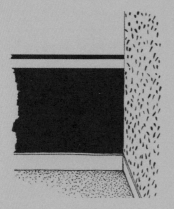

PROJECT ONE

PROJECT TWO

painted dado stripe

By Cassie Nicholas, as seen in Series 1, episode 8

Create an alternative dado rail while retaining perfectly flat walls through strategic use of paint. Mask off the lower third of your wall and paint this in a contrasting colour to the top two thirds. Leaving the masking tape in place, add a second strip a few centimetres (around an inch) above this, then paint the slim gap between the two in the same colour as your lower walls. Remove all masking tape before the paint dries. For a less structured look, you could paint your dado stripe freehand, embracing the natural wobbles and imperfections.

deconstructed chandelier

By Charlotte Beevor, as seen in Series 2, episode 3

For a playful approach to the classic ceiling rose, install a multi-wired pendant light, positioning each flex at different points across your ceiling, but add new ceiling roses into the spaces in between them rather than suspending the flex directly from them. Turn off your power supply before installing the central light fitting, following the manufacturer's instructions. The decorative roses that aren't supporting any light fittings can simply be glued directly to the ceiling using an appropriate polymer joint adhesive (assuming you choose a modern lightweight polyurethane design).

Whether you are decorating a period property or not, try out these fun projects which blend vintage style with modern aesthetics.

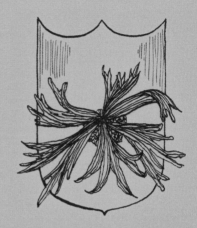

PROJECT THREE

PROJECT FOUR

bedhead panelling

By Frank Newbold, as seen in Series 1, episode 1

Nodding to period wall panelling, these upholstered fabric inserts create a contemporary headboard. Work out your preferred size for each insert, then cut a rectangular MDF panel to that size. Use spray mount to fix some same-size upholstery foam to its front, then cover it with fabric, pulled taught and secured on its underside with staples. Fix onto your walls using screws in the corners, or (if it's fairly lightweight) wood glue. To create the frame, fix a low skirting board trim to the walls (large enough to snugly fit each panel), mitre cutting each corner for a seamless fit (see pages 218–221 for more upholstery advice).

mounted staghorn fern

By Banjo Beale, as seen in Series 3, episode 7

Introduce a twist on the traditional mounted stag head using a staghorn fern. Buy a wooden shield trophy plate (or cut your own using a coping saw) that will amply accommodate the fern's roots. Hammer multiple nails in a circle through the front of the plate, slightly wider than the fern's base, leaving them protruding around 1cm (¼in). Laying it flat, pile on a small amount of compost, add your fern to the top so its roots touch the soil, then place pieces of sheet moss across the exposed soil. Use fishing wire to wind around each nail, working across the board, until the root/moss base is fully secure, then hang on a sawtooth picture hanger.

Style school

fads vs trends

Does flipping through an interiors magazine or watching your favourite TV design show (ahem) sometimes leave you feeling more overwhelmed than inspired? It can be very easy to get swept up by the latest trends and lose track of your personal design compass. With a little guidance you'll be able to navigate this path and find your own way through, gaining inspiration from ideas that make your heart sing.

The word 'trend' is really an umbrella term, relating to a general lifestyle shift or movement – our growing collective interest in sustainability, for example, has resulted in a resurgence of more planet-friendly materials like cork, rattan and bamboo. And while the schemes these materials end up being used in could turn into shorter-term trends and even fads, the overriding rationale behind using them isn't likely to fall out of fashion. Always keep in mind the bigger picture of what's important to you as a useful steer.

It can be helpful to think in terms of 'themes' versus 'concepts' if you feel your design might be in danger of falling into the fad category. A theme is often a very faithful interpretation of a particular look – for example, a nautical scheme that features pebble ornaments and anchor motif wallpaper; a more conceptual space might incorporate rough hessian textures, bleached woods and organic, rounded side tables, none of which scream 'seaside', yet all gently nod to the typical materials and

finishes you'd expect to find by the coast. The latter is more about the relationships between the pieces and the environment they are in (or that has inspired them), and while this look might be considered 'trendy' at times, it isn't slavishly following a trend and should therefore offer more longevity as a design (as well as being easier to amend as tastes change).

Bear in mind that when magazines photograph decorating features, they are creating a hyper-stylised interpretation of a trend, designed to inspire and inform you on the directions the industry is headed in. They are not necessarily intended to be copied wholesale, and doing so can result in schemes that might look great on camera, but don't resonate in reality.

The following pages aim to demystify the basic premise and principles of a number of different design trends, but with an emphasis on how you can interpret and combine these to give them your own unique twist and develop your signature style with aunthenticity.

'When I got the brief of "coastal style" in episode 5 for my shepherd's hut makeover (seen above), Michelle [Ogundehin] advised me to avoid the typical coastal cliches. I wanted to understand what the coastline was like in this area: it's beautiful, but it changes in an instant, it certainly isn't all white sandy beaches and blue skies. To reflect this, I wanted my design to be moody, rugged and not like a typical seaside holiday kind of theme.'

Banjo Beale, Design Contestant, Series 3

'My style is slightly over the top and I don't tend to follow trends that much. I don't necessarily want to design spaces that everyone's going to love, I want to design for those few people who are really going to love it. And I love being that hands-on person who just tries things out.'

Cassie Nicholas, Design Contestant, Series 1

Design styles and signature styles

heritage

When it comes to interiors, 'heritage' generally refers to the designs and architectural styles that emerged during the 19th and early 20th centuries. While it's a term more commonly associated with buildings of historical or cultural importance, as with all design there is a trickle-down effect (because why *shouldn't* you borrow aesthetic influences from grand stately homes just because you live in a two-bed new-build?).

Great design is always an evolution in one way or another, borrowing ideas from the past while giving them a new twist to keep things current. Heritage style leans heavily on the nostalgic ideas of traditional sturdy building stock and strong British values (though, of course, this will be felt differently by those whose own heritage comes from different countries and cultures). It also harks back to a time when craftsmanship was king, before mass production overtook the handmade, and homes were decorated with natural and handcrafted pieces.

Keep the concept of design discipline in mind when mixing together lots of different styles and eras: while heritage style can lean towards eccentricity (which can be a wonderfully fun and flamboyant way to decorate), simply throwing together different 'crazy' design elements without getting to grips with your underlying palette, theme or ideas can end up feeling chaotic rather than avant-garde.

How to make it your own

Country charm

- Borrow ideas from 'heritage-with-a-country-twist' establishments like Soho Farmhouse and The Pig Hotel, who effortlessly mix touches of quiet grandeur with more humble design details (think a baroque gilt-framed oil painting hanging above a vintage butcher's block, or a velvet armchair paired with a battered old leather Chesterfield).
- Scour online auction sites for vintage fabrics that are a little faded, for character. Many modern fabric patterns are printed directly onto a fabric's surface, while more traditional methods of pattern creation can suit period schemes better: look for designs created by wood block or silkscreen printing, or for woven patterns such as damask or brocade over digital reproductions.
- Keep colours muted, mid-toned and nature inspired: think sage greens, warm browns, and the odd pop of russet red to break things up.

Gentlemen's club

- As the name suggests, this masculine style favours the dark, sleek and interesting (though isn't afraid of a pattern or two). It can also incorporate a touch of Art Deco, from curved furniture arms to touches of gold as accents. Think dark, glossy floors, a moody colour palette and luxe materials such as marble tabletops and leather wingback chairs.
- Keep to more structured patterns like houndstooth and geometric prints, letting the shapes of your furniture do the talking.
- Bring in a Mid-century twist by swapping out the stag heads and roaring fires for a more pared back *Mad Men* vibe, with simplified details that still nod to heritage glamour.

Conservatory chic

- Whether you've got a sprawling orangery or simply an armchair by a small sunny window, create a plant-filled nook that nods towards the Victorian obsession with botany: ferns, palms and begonias were all hugely popular and have a nostalgic quality. Wardian cases (which create a closed terrarium environment) offer another nod to the style.
- Bring foliage and flowers onto walls with prints, or by pressing your own specimens and displaying them in glass-backed frames.

- Up for some serious pattern? Go immersive with a classic foliage wallpaper design, then paint ceilings and woodwork in a tonally related colour to tie the whole look together. Choosing items with black metal accents (say furniture legs) will allude to the wrought iron used in the construction of Victorian conservatories.

'In my eyes, Britishness in design is a kind of irreverence; it's about that island mentality of pushing against the norm – we're the home of punk and yet we also do classic and traditional really well. It's about that contrast.'

Michelle Ogundehin

MICAELA AND SIOBHAN'S ART DECO SEATING NOOK

Tasked with renovating a traditional barber shop within an Art Deco building (Series 2, episode 7), Siobhan and Micaela wanted to show how you can respect a building's heritage while still introducing contemporary twists.

'The owners wanted an Art Deco/speakeasy/ gentlemen's club vibe. I'm so pleased with how it turned out ... it's got such a nice energy, it's pretty magical.'

Siobhan Murphy, Design Contestant, Series 2

'There's a fusion here between mine and Siobhan's elements. We certainly hit the brief's requirements for the style, but the feel is something you either have or you don't – and it's definitely a lovely space.'

Micaela Sharp, Design Contestant, Series 2

The space

Using a dark colour palette and three different wallpapers, the design duo
opted to mix 1930s designs and patterns (to complement the bones of this
Art Deco space) with older Victorian references, as a nod to the heyday
of the traditional barber shop. This was achieved by mixing in subtle
elements of gold and glitz with darker apothecary-style design details,
such as Victorian-inspired cabinetry. Featuring reds and burgundies as
their dominant colours, they also used dark browns and heritage greens
as accents to temper the whole look.

For the seating area within the barber's, a homely look was created
with a customised sofa, painted coffee table and an antique cabinet, used
for both storage and display.

Get the look

+   Hanging wallpaper on the
diagonal gives a very different
look to going horizontal or
vertical, especially with graphic
patterns. This technique could
also work using a single strip
to cut through a painted wall,
as an alternative.

+   To give a diffused glow,
decorative glass ceiling shades
were used to cover existing
spotlights, visually softening
them. Each shade was hung directly
beneath each spotlight, its metal
hanging chains suspended from
small cup hooks in the ceiling,
offering an easy way to create a
new lighting look without actually
touching the electrics. This can
be a great option for kitchen or
bathroom spaces, where spotlights
are often the most practical
option, yet they may not suit
your vibe.

+   The burgundy paint selected
for the main interior walls, made
to order at an in-store paint
mixing station, ended up being much
lighter in appearance than Siobhan
was hoping for: to remedy this and
save on the cost of replacing it,
she added an extra shot of black
paint to the tin to darken and mute
it. While this is a wise option
when you're in a bind, bear in mind
that if you run out, this could
lead to issues when you try to
match up a new batch (if in doubt,
order a sample pot first!).

+   Be brave and play with colours
that are on the cusp of clashing:
Micaela and Siobhan created visual
friction by pairing a bold red and
white striped wallpaper with a more
intricate Deco-inspired pattern
which had a burgundy base. While it
might not be everyone's cup of tea,
design-wise it works due to the
tonal relation (the burgundy falls

within the red arc of the colour wheel), and by choosing two very different designs - rather than busy, conflicting patterns - there's no visual battle for dominance.

+ When shopping for second-hand furniture, remember to envisage how something could be, rather than how it necessarily is right now. Micaela bought this slightly worn second-hand sofa from an online auction site for just £1; by adding velvet tops to the damaged seat cushion covers, she created a bespoke look for next to nothing. With its Deco-inspired arms, it fitted the scheme to perfection.

'I'm loving this masculine, reduced colour palette - it feels really considered. The lighting is clever, with little pockets of glow in amongst practical lighting, which is nice ... it's a really confident design.'

Abigail Ahern, Interior Designer and Guest Judge

'The exciting possibilities of design really open up when you dare to dream - when you're confident about your choices and take on board all the inspiration around you.'

Michelle Ogundehin

give your sofa cushion covers a glow-up

+ Remove your seat cushion covers from their cushion inserts, and turn inside out. Using a seam ripper, remove all the stitching from the top of the seat cover then use this top piece as your template, cutting out your replacement fabric to the same shape and size.

+ With your new fabric pattern-side down, line this up with the seams on the now-empty top of the cover, so it sits where the previous fabric was. Pin around the edges, then sew it back into position along the original stitching lines using a sewing machine (or by hand, if you're patient!).

+ Once complete, turn inside out again so it's now the right way out, then reinsert your cushion pad. Repeat for each seat cover - you might want to mix it up with different fabrics, or stick with the same for a uniform look.

industrial

Industrial style can be thought of as the somewhat cooler cousin of Victorian design. While typical homes of the same era were filled with fussy, busy patterns and designs, their commercial counterpart spaces were in contrast far simpler and more utilitarian. Yet – Victorians being Victorians – these factories, warehouses and office buildings still contained decorative flourishes, such as patterned glazed tiles, decorative brickwork and Gothic arches, and their generous steel-framed windows and spaciousness has made the look increasingly desirable for domestic living.

Even if you live in a suburban semi, there are plenty of ways to bring a little industrial chic into your home – here are a few ideas.

How to make it your own

Luxe-industrial

- Industrial looks needn't mean rough textures or clinical surfaces: bring in a sense of glam by incorporating warmer materials such as copper leaf or cladding, and gold accents like handles with a knurled finish (where the surface is textured with cross-hatched indentations). Sculptural accessories made from sheet metal will look stylish and contemporary, referencing the industrial look in a more subtle way.
- Upgrade any glass cupboard or glazed doors with some reeded glass film. Most designs are inexpensive and easy to apply, and offer an instant industrial twist while also adding privacy and interest.
- Dark colour palettes complement industrial style: play around with paint finishes and add some high-shine gloss accents to bounce the light around and bring a touch of drama.

Warehouse vibes

- In older properties, you might be lucky enough to find charming London stock bricks lurking under plasterboard: these can look stunning exposed, but will likely require treatment such as painting with a clear matte PVA bond to stop them dropping dust. For newer properties, a brick slip tile can be applied for a facsimile look.
- Undertaking an extension? See if you can incorporate exposed RSJs (rolled steel joists) into your design. Used to add support where structural or load-bearing walls have been removed, these usually come finished in red oxide, but if left exposed rather than boxed in will need treating with fire-retardant intumescent paint (this is easy to apply yourself, and you can add your own paint on top).
- Cheat the look of Crittall-style windows by adding some faux panes to existing glazing by using a thin strip of black

electrical tape, applied to both sides of the glass, which can be easily moved if misaligned.

Industrial farmhouse

- We tend to think of countryside homes as rustic (and possibly twee), but many industrial spaces end up being converted into domestic residences and manage to successfully marry industrial elements with a homely space.

- Layer in industrial materials as backdrops: corrugated sheeting can be used as a decorative wall cladding or turned into a room partition, adding texture and interest. Source panels with authentic ageing from a salvage yard, or, to give it a luxe look, paint new sheeting with a flexible acrylic paint that will accommodate the natural movement of the surface. Stainless steel brings a no-nonsense practicality to kitchen worktops and domestic tables.

- Look at the details, too: copper pipe can be turned into cool, utilitarian taps (ask your local plumber to create these), or used to create a hanging rail in a kitchen (just add S-hooks); industrial gate valve handles can be used in place of drawer pulls or door handles for a fun accent.

'I like to juxtapose decorations with a high sheen finish against the rougher textures of bare brick or concrete – a polished brass Danish lamp, for example, could give some much needed warmth to a room, as can the earthy palette of unglazed ceramics in light clay or terracotta colours.'

Karl Mok, Design Contestant, Series 4

AMY'S RUSTIC-LUXE LODGE

Amy's treatment for this getaway riverside lodge (Series 3, episode 7) blended elements of industrial design with some Scandi-chic and rustic influences, to create a look that offered a pared-back, contemporary yet still cosy space to relax, unwind and socialise. Her 'harder' elements – black woodwork contrasted with crisp white walls – were softened with limestone-toned accents, raw wood, faux foliage and buttery soft leather sofas for a blended look.

'The brief here was for something modern, contemporary and grown-up, which is quite pared back compared to my usual style... I've played to all my strengths and tried things I wouldn't normally do – I've not relied on masses of colour or my usual quirks. I feel like I'm not just a print designer anymore, I can do the whole thing.'

Amy Davies, Design Contestant, Series 3

The space

Amy opted to switch around the open-plan layout of this soaring duplex living space to bring in a better sense of flow, moving the dining area so it was adjacent to the kitchen (and leading directly through to the outdoor sofa on the decking beyond), giving a cosier, more contained feel to the living area, now at the other end of the space.

Get the look

+ Painting the existing naturally finished woodwork (around the window frames and on the exposed wooden stair treads) nodded to an industrial metal look while also framing the outside view. Primer is your friend for recreating this look at home: you can even get the look on uPVC frames if using the correct primer and topcoat. Ask your local decorating centre what the most suitable product is for your surface.

+ The existing kitchen peninsula was reimagined as a fun bar space for breakfast (or cocktails!), and its construction - from reclaimed wooden boards - was chosen to contrast with the otherwise slick, glossy kitchen units. Get this look by cutting two boards to size: one the length of the peninsula worktop, and the other the height from the floor to the existing worktop plus the height of the new board. Mitre these two corners together for a neat fit, then place this so the front third rests on the existing worktop while the back overhangs the redundant space behind it, creating a space for

bar stools. Secure into position using brackets underneath the overhanging wood.

+ Create a pick-your-own-herbs bar above a dining table, as a fun talking point and a novel way to season your meals. Suspend a hanging gantry or wire frame from the ceiling on metal chains using cup hooks, being mindful to secure them into joists for strength, then suspend pots of herbs from this. You can buy hanging pots and baskets, or customise an existing pot by tying string around its rim: tie three additional strings to this, knotting them together at the top, then this can hang from an S-hook on your gantry. Try weaving some faux flowers through the wire frame to soften the look, as Amy did. Bear in mind that herbs need six to eight hours of solid sunlight each day to grow, so unless your dining table is in a particularly sunny spot, they may need additional support from an LED grow light.

create your own: woodland bookcase

+ Install some simple floating bookshelves onto your wall: black or white laminate will work well to give this look some industrial-influenced contrast (follow the fitting instructions they come with to secure in place).

+ Source some rustic poles or branches: these should be sturdy, but they're not offering structural support so go with the look you want. Speak to your local salvage timber merchant to see if they have anything suitable, or simply go foraging for fallen branches.

+ Once you've gathered your wood, cut it with a hand saw so you can snugly insert each length between the ends of each shelf, to look like the branch is growing through them. The shelves should hold them into position, but for extra security you could add a blob of strong wood adhesive to either end first.

'Here, we've got the contemporary with some rustic touches. Adding this lovely old bit of wood to create a breakfast bar, which could otherwise feel a bit hard and masculine, gives you that mix and balance between rough and smooth that we need.'

Michelle Ogundehin

'There's just a beautiful synergy here which I think is really quite clever. She's very good at – and I think this is a hard thing to nail – getting friction into interiors, so it just looks beautiful but not silly. And I love how she's carried the black throughout the whole space ... what's especially clever is the friction between both old and contemporary materials. It looks really considered.'

Abigail Ahern, Interior Designer and Guest Judge

minimal

Minimal style is often touted as hugely and enduringly popular, but it's a surprisingly difficult look to pull off and often people's interpretations of what minimal means can be quite different from a genuinely minimalist scheme.

In its truest form, minimalism favours clean lines, a tightly controlled colour palette (usually devoid of strong colours), and a focus on fewer possessions – ensuring those 'lucky few' that get picked are worthy of being considered statement pieces. Yet it can easily tip into feeling cold, stark and unwelcoming if not handled with care. It's also important not to confuse 'minimalism' with 'clutter/pattern-free': yes, you might prefer a plainer space without clutter in full view, but this can be quite a different proposition to living in a space that contains only a few highly edited prized possessions of artistic merit. So if you like the idea of simpler living but aren't quite ready to shed your worldly goods and live in a white box, try twisting it a little and experiment with the right balance to suit both your practical needs and desire for less (visual and mental) clutter in your life.

How to make it your own

Shaker style

– With utopian roots, the Shaker style could almost be thought of as a relaxed, country-inspired style of minimalism, with simple, hardworking pieces at its core. Bringing in fuss-free furnishings made from natural materials nods to this look, while introducing tactility.

– If you want clutter-free living without getting rid of too many possessions, borrow some Shaker-style storage ideas: their much-copied peg rail is easy to install at eye level/picture rail height and can be useful in all rooms, from kid's bedrooms to bathrooms. Team with simple woven baskets or string shoppers to maximise their usefulness.

– Give a Shaker-inspired twist to flat-fronted cupboard doors by drilling holes in place of cabinet pulls, and adding in a few more to add simple patterns to the door fronts (which is also good for ventilation). Use a hole saw attachment on a corded drill, then sand any rough edges.

Organic warmth

– Avoid the stark look sometimes associated with minimalism by banishing pure whites and opting instead for warmer tones like putty, greige and taupe: they all sit along the same tonal spectrum, yet work in a more harmonious way.

– Nature doesn't really do right angles, so choose furniture and accessories that are rounded off rather than containing sharp corners.

- Texture is your friend when it comes to bringing warmth to a scheme: play around and even exaggerate it by incorporating long-pile flokati rugs, natural wool throws on chairs and beds, and loose-weave linens at windows.

Cheeky accents

- While bright colour pops aren't in the spirit of true minimalism, if you'd prefer a more hybrid look, consider adding subtle accents of a vibrant hue to an otherwise pared-back and simple scheme to give a little visual friction. Keeping it confined to smaller areas, like lighting cables or a statement art print, will make it pop out from an otherwise pale scheme.
- Textured surfaces offer another way to bring in a subtle form of accent: choose tiles or cupboard doors with graphic carved details or an embossed effect, letting the shadows they create do the talking.
- If you like the occasional hit of bright colour but don't want to be surrounded with it all the time, confine it to usually hidden areas, like the inside of cupboard doors. You'll be able to enjoy your serene space when you need that visual rest, yet be occasionally hit with a dopamine-inducing bright throughout the day.

'Life is chaotic and at times we all crave a sense of relaxation in our homes to help diffuse the chaos of the outside world. Clutter is a major factor that can slow down the process of healing: when designing a space, I like to hide away everything that I don't want to be seen, and show off just the items I find most beautiful, to create a feeling of easy living while still maintaining easy access to the essentials.

I tend to avoid loud patterns and colours as they don't support the calming narrative I personally prefer. I like to use earthy shades in similar tones to achieve natural depth in the space. And to replace pattern, I use texture to create a variety of subtle moments in a space. Mixing raw wood with tactile rope, timeless linen and airy grasses all brings points of difference without having to rely on louder aesthetic touches.'

Peter Irvine, *Design Contestant*, Series 4

Design styles and signature styles

CASSIE'S SHAKER-INFLUENCED LIVING ROOM

Cassie successfully brought a pared-back aesthetic – with her trademark boho twist – to the open-plan living area of her residential apartment redesign (Series 1, episode 8). Artfully blending a Shaker-style display wall with restrained yet luxe accents, while incorporating vintage furniture and reclaimed materials, resulted in a warm and characterful end result.

The space

Situated in a converted industrial building, this open-plan layout required thoughtful zoning that could also accommodate changing requirements for the whole family throughout the day. As such, this battened wall detail was generously added across one entire wall, allowing for the display of decorative accessories nearer the entrance and dining space, and more practical storage for a TV and books within the lounge area.

Get the look

+   Minimalist style is as much about paying special attention to the quality of the smallest details as it is about the whole space. Bringing in gold accents can help create a polished, considered look, especially when pairing them with more rustic surfaces like wood. A spritz of gold spray paint is a great way to elevate any existing decorative ornaments.

+   To recreate this battened wall, use 100x100mm (4x4in) wooden posts to form your uprights, and some lengths of shallow timber to form your shelves. Screw the first of your upright posts to your wall, from the floor (or skirting) up to the height you'd like your first shelf, then glue and screw your shelf to the top ends of the uprights. Repeat with the next set of uprights and shelf until your whole wall is clad.

+   To create an uncluttered feel without things feeling bare, introduce vintage furniture and accessories which are simple in design yet have an imperfect patina. Antique and vintage pieces, like these classic cane weave dining chairs, help to bring character while sharing the overall industrial aesthetic of this space.

+   If you're aiming to blend other styles with minimalist principles, watch for mixed design metaphors.

Here, there's a shared language in the bigger pieces and the accent details: geometric shapes like the subtle chevron pattern in the tabletop are nodded to in the vase, and the hexagonal pattern in the cane weave chairs is referenced in the industrial-style overhead light.

'This wall is very clever, and unexpected.'
Matthew Williamson, Interior Designer and Guest Judge

'It feels very balanced: everything sits well together, which it has to do in an open-plan space. And it's great having this sneaky shelving – it makes the whole wall useful.' Michelle Ogundehin

'I wanted to give my client something that they might not have done themselves, but that they'd really love. If they'd got exactly what they had hoped for, I don't think I'd have quite done my job – I wanted to give them a bit more.' Cassie Nicholas, Design Contestant, Series 1

See pages 212–213 for practical advice on panelling your walls.

rustic

Arguably one of the broadest design styles, rustic is a term often attributed to many different looks, from weather-worn Mediterranean villas to cosy cottages. In fact, you could put a rustic twist on most of the styles featured in this chapter. But in essence, the look can be considered one of faded beauty, championing honest, characterful materials in a laid-back setting.

Though it's a look that originated organically and isn't tied to a specific country or time period, there are many ways to tap into this authentic aesthetic and it can be a great way to add character to newer properties (or older spaces lacking in original period features).

How to make it your own

Cabin chic

- Who *wouldn't* like a bolt-hole hideaway in the woods? If you love the look but not so much the wilderness aspect, bring the style into your home instead. Adding wood cladding to walls is a great place to start; seek out old floorboards from a salvage yard, or use reclaimed pallet wood, which you can build up in a slightly more patchwork design (both of which could potentially be collected for free if you're prepared to rummage in a few neighbourhood skips, though do ask permission before taking). See pages 214–215 for ways to install it.
- Consider going super-dark and bring in some shou sugi ban, a Japanese wood charring treatment traditionally used to darken wooden timbers and make them weatherproof. Typically used on cedar to clad building exteriors, the technique can also work on internally clad timbers (it is essential to apply this treatment before installation, in a well-ventilated outdoor setting) and even on furniture like wooden tabletops. A blow torch will be your best bet, though do check with a professional first to ensure your set-up and wood type is suitable.
- For an 'urban cabin' twist (great for a garden summerhouse), contrast with contemporary straight-edged wooden furniture accents and keep styling fairly minimal, or for an up-in-the-mountains vibe, layer in fur throws and lots of accent lighting.

Coastal style

- Incorporating materials like Cotswold stone brings warmth and tactility, nodding to shingle beaches and cobbled coastal streets. Using natural slate, limestone or terracotta floor tiles equally gives this subtle inference.
- Swap the rustic wood cladding for a (visually and physical) lighter tongue-and-

groove panelled wall. If your walls aren't in great shape, consider building this out slightly on wooden battens attached to the walls, rather than onto the walls themselves; you can then add a slim ledge on top for displaying artworks and small trinkets.

– Bring in rustic woven textures like rattan and rope, to reference the beach without being too literal. Could you replace any ugly on-show storage boxes with alternatives made from these forgiving materials?

Make it modern

– Exposed wooden beams on ceilings is a look often associated with rustic spaces, and brings with it a natural charm. It's easy for this to look pastiche outside of a traditional cottage setting, but if you've got an interesting, sloped ceiling in a new extension, consider using modern timber to add more minimalist decorative beams, painted the same colour as ceilings or kept to a simple limewash.

– Elaborately aged paint effects on furniture can feel a bit over-egged, but wooden pieces do a great job of alluding to a rustic style. To keep it modern, consider painting vintage pieces in a bold, contemporary colour, or switch out original handles for a new alternative.

– Contrast all your matte, earthy finishes with the odd bit of subtle sheen. A hammered metal drum coffee table or aged copper splashback will be a little more in keeping than something super-glitzy, however.

'I enjoy making homewares from willow, which I collect locally. I used this approach to create various lampshades in a few different rooms I designed on the show. The full steps would make for a long tutorial, but a fun way to add your own (literal) spin on weaving is to take any type of basket or woven vessel and weave through some rope. It might be that you have to remove some existing willow or rattan to replace with rope or jute, but the structure is there, and you are just adding another interesting element.'

Banjo Beale, Design Contestant, Series 3

JU AND NICKI'S COSY CHALET

Nicki and Ju collaborated to create a rustic-influenced space (Series 1, episode 5) that still retained elements of their signature fresh, bright styles, resulting in a design which felt soft and delicate, yet robust and rooted in nature.

The space

Although set in a beautiful countryside location overlooking a fishing lake, this brand-new lodge was somewhat lacking in character, and also - aside from that all-important view - had no focal space. Ju and Nicki's brief - to create a home-from-home luxury retreat that reflected its immediate surroundings and woodland setting - led them to create a cosy, country-casual seating area, surrounded with textures and accessories that reflected the overall environment.

Get the look

+   Adding simple vertical timber cladding across all the interior walls nods to traditional wainscoting, but with a contemporary twist (and using only vertical battens takes a lot less labour and time to install than full panelling). Painting the lower third of the walls in a dark tone also alludes to a traditional dado rail, without the fiddly fixings.

+   Installing a faux fireplace on a flat wall (here, set in between two picture windows) gives an additional focal point and, by using chunky timbers to form the surround, brings a characterful feel. If you need to mount your TV above a fireplace, soften the look by adding lots of textural plants and ornaments along both the mantel top and the hearth area.

+   Have fun with accessories that playfully reference your design theme or the surrounding area: Nicki and Ju went to town bringing in lots of vintage fishing baskets (doubling as storage) and even creating a talking-point floor lamp from an old fishing rod, fixed upright and wrapped with a plug-in pendant light set.

'This just goes to show you what design can achieve – adding this delicious panelling gives everything a bit more articulation ... This set-up faces the view, so I'm starting from a happy place. I rather like the two-toned wall because it picks up the line of the kitchen (the kitchen's base units are painted the same colour) so when you're sitting, it gives an extra little detail.'

Michelle Ogundehin

'Having a big, squishy sofa overlooking the view is really lovely, but one of my pet peeves is cutting the wall in half with one colour – I think it makes a space feel closed-in. But that's a personal thing.'

Abigail Ahern, Interior Designer and Guest Judge

'For this project, I really listened to the advice Michelle gave me in terms of editing myself and my ideas, but without compromising on design.'

Nicki Bamford-Bowes, Design Contestant, Series 1

florals

While dropping in and out of fashion over the decades (and indeed centuries), floral patterns are generally always in vogue in one form or another (and even when they're not, plenty of people still use them anyway). Over the last half-century or so, things have gone full circle, with nostalgic and twee 1950s prints becoming wildly popular among younger generations who are discovering them for the first time, after their traditional looks fell firmly out of favour for much of the '90s and '00s.

Floral prints can carry an unfair stigma of being old-fashioned, yet they come in an incredibly broad range of styles – from acid-bright Pop-art inspired designs to gentle pastoral scenes, via full-on Victoriana (which inspired Swedish retailer IKEA to shout at us Brits to 'chuck out our chintz' in its trend-shifting 1996 campaign). Increasingly, they're also being used in dark and moody schemes, with classic archival prints being released in contemporary new colourways.

How to make it your own

Cottagecore

- Coined on social media, the cottagecore trend has proved popular for several years and shows no signs of fading, indicating that it's far more than just a passing fad. A backlash against busy urban living, it romanticises a simple rural lifestyle filled with flowers and farmers markets, bringing with it a maximalist aesthetic.
- Floral prints closely represent nature, and favour looser country-style flowers over anything overly 'posh' and curated. This humble feel pairs well with equally simple materials: think printed cotton, mismatched vintage crockery and the odd bit of tassel fringing.
- Temper your floral prints with farmhouse-inspired basics like simple vintage wooden furniture, artisan-made ceramics and hand-crafted objet. For a fully farmhouse vibe, bring in other cottage-style elements, such as terracotta tiled floors and wood-panelled walls, or for contrast, introduce a little luxe with velvets and satins.

Painterly blooms

- Oversized artistic floral designs are a great way to make a statement across walls or soft furnishing, from more abstract designs to rich oil painting-inspired prints.
- Go super-scale with a mural: these bolder designs work wonderfully in larger formats, and it can also give a more contemporary overall look. You can order bespoke murals to fit your wall online, or, if you're feeling arty, try creating one yourself with tester paint pots (see pages

206–207 for guidance).

- Introduce complementary painterly elements, such as loose painted stripes in accent details, spatterware crockery sets, or ceramic accessories featuring double-dipped glazes.

Folksy florals

- With no set definition, folk art prints are generally considered to be of and for ordinary people, rather than created by trained artists as the preserve of only the wealthy. Folksy florals tend to feature naive, stylistic (rather than realistic) prints in a medley of natural-toned pigments.

- Bring in block- and screen-printed materials to retain a sense of authenticity, sticking with a colour palette that feels true to nature (so lots of greens and earthy tones punctuated by a few vibrant colour pops).

- These charming details work well paired with more geometric-style block prints, or ikat patterned fabrics (created by resist-dyeing yarn before weaving striking patterns directly into the fabric).

'There is a real knack to creating an eclectic interior and ensuring that it doesn't look mismatched or chaotic. Pick a bold, contrasting colour palette, then choose one element throughout the whole scheme that ties it together – something subtle that runs the whole way through the design to give the look intentionality and cohesion. This could be the use of a certain material; for example a stone side table next to a sofa, then add a stone lamp base to a sideboard and a stone ornament on a shelf. It could also be choosing one pattern that follows through the space in textiles, like a rug, lampshade and cushion.'

Molly Coath, Design Contestant, Series 3

Design styles and signature styles

FRAN'S MODERN FLORAL BEDROOM

While on the lookout for a showstopping wallpaper for her hotel bedroom redesign (Series 3, episode 2), Fran found this glorious print which not only fitted her vision but also worked for the 'British eccentric' theme each design contestant was given. To rebalance the budget, she added paint effects to the hotel's existing mock-antique furniture and made her own oversized statement lampshade, for an other-worldly vibe.

'I've channelled Kate Middleton cool, but also taken inspiration from the Arts and Crafts movement and William Morris. I've got some beautiful floral wallpaper, which was about a third of my budget, that was my starting point for the whole scheme. With my statement ceiling light, I wanted a "wow" light fitting without the "wow-that's-scary" price tag, so this is the result. I wanted to keep the space modern and fresh, rather than looking like it's a set from Downton Abbey.'

Fran Lee, Design Contestant, Series 3

The space

As a generously sized bedroom with large, vaulted ceilings, this room needed an equally bold focal point, which Fran's wallpaper provided. She also introduced floral details throughout the space, seen in her patterned lamp bases and a vase of freshly cut meadow flowers from the grounds outside, to integrate florals into the whole room with a light touch.

Get the look

+   If, like Fran, you're painting over faux wood furniture (which is usually coated in a plastic-based melamine or laminate), and you're keen to create an aged, shabby-chic finish, opt for chalk paint; you can apply it directly to these types of surfaces without needing to prime or sand first, and by building up the brushstrokes you can create that perfectly imperfect look (you'll just need to wax it at the end, for durability). Fran used a mix of off-white and blue chalk paints on her bedroom pieces, dry brushing more of the off-white over her blue dressing table, for a coastal nod.

+   Add a touch of boho-chic to a basic fabric lampshade by covering the whole thing in fringing trim. Start at the back of the shade, where its seam is, then use a hot glue gun to fix the back of the trim to the shade, working in sections until the whole piece is covered.

+   When you're creating an eclectic look, check in with yourself to make sure your enthusiasm for your scheme isn't sending your overall vision in the wrong direction: is everything still speaking the same design language?

+   To bring a cosy, layered look to your bed, mix in different textures, like a shiny satin quilted bedspread with a more grounding linen throw on top. Then layer on cushions in different sizes, designs and formats as accents.

create your own: papier-mâché lampshade

+ Blow up a balloon to the size you'd like your finished lampshade to be (giant round ones work well for statement shades) and hang it upside down from a stable support, with a protective sheet on the floor around it.

+ Taking some torn strips of newspaper and a bowl of watered down PVA glue, dip in the paper strips one at a time then begin layering them onto the top half of the balloon, leaving the edge slightly uneven for an organic look. Build up until it's well covered, then leave to dry (depending on depth of layers, it can take up to 24 hours to fully dry).

+ Pop the balloon and remove any remaining plastic, then cut a hole in the top to accommodate your light fitting. Give the exterior a coat of emulsion paint in a colour of your choosing. For added glitz, use a metallic spray paint to coat the interior, which will reflect the light when switched on. Once everything is dry, fix it onto your light fitting: make sure you use an LED bulb so it doesn't generate heat and - for safety - glue a metal reducer ring plate to the top of the inside, to ensure the metal of your light fitting isn't directly touching the paper.

'This is a really sophisticated wallpaper – I love its colour palette. But when you walk into the room, you walk in to a green painted wall (with the wallpaper to your back) and I do think it should have been the other way round. I really like the ceiling light, it's chic and modern, and I like the painterly finish she's added to her furniture.'

Guy Oliver, Interior Designer and Guest Judge

'This light is a great statement – I love the effect of the gold used in its interior.'

Michelle Ogundehin

Scandi

Britain's love affair with Scandinavian style (designs derived from Norway, Sweden and Denmark) dates back to the 1950s, when the term was coined. Despite its roots harking back to the 19th century, its wholly modernist aesthetic was greeted by an audience enthralled by this contemporary new style, with its focus on clean lines and practical, ergonomically designed pieces.

Crucially, its simply shaped furnishings, typically created from inexpensive pale woods like beech, ash and pine, made it very viable for mass production, allowing a broader range of budgets to bring the look into their homes. In keeping with this pale and simple aesthetic (and as a result of their often long, dark winters), Scandinavians tend to greatly value light and space, opting for clutter-free floors and sparse, simple decor; though to avoid feeling stark, homes will also typically feature natural materials like stone, wood, fur and leather.

How to make it your own

Japandi

- If a purely pale space isn't for you, consider a 'Japandi' approach: a portmanteau of Japanese and Scandinavian design aesthetics, this look brings in dark charcoal tones to temper an otherwise pale scheme, placing emphasis on the curves of furniture and accent details to carry through a visual softness.
- Japanese spaces are well known for making use of screens to divide up larger open-plan spaces; integrating some into your own home can help visually separate different areas. Traditional shoji-style screens are often made from thick, translucent paper stretched across a lattice wooden frame – search for similar styles here in the UK online.
- Bamboo is commonly grown and used in Japan, and its warm, light wood fits in well with a Scandi aesthetic, too. As a sustainable and sturdy grass material, it's a great alternative to wood for furniture, flooring and accessories.

Lagom

- More of a concept than an aesthetic, the Swedish word lagom translates roughly as 'not too much, not too little', and can be used as a guiding principle when choosing any colours, patterns (or lack thereof) and accessories.
- When taking a sparing approach to your home's design, you want your choices to be good ones: consider investing in some Danish design classics (shop second-hand for potential bargains) from iconic designers such as Hans Wegner, Arne Jacobsen and Verner Panton.

- Sweden has an esteemed glass-blowing industry dating back to the 18th century: bringing in a few authentic hand-blown ornaments from stalwart Swedish makers is a great way to add subtle statement accessories.

Hygge

- Despite reaching peak press saturation a few years ago, hygge certainly shouldn't be written off as a fad, with the concept dating back to the 1800s. Loosely translated as being a quality of cosiness, contentment and conviviality, this could arguably be accentuated by a number of different design styles (or indeed none at all), though it's often associated with cosy armchairs, lots of layers and a sociable layout.

- Layered lighting is helpful in aiding hygge. Try to have a few different sources together for a cosy feel, from wall and table lamps to string lights and candles. It's all about that warm glow (cosy atmospheres are much harder to conjure up under harsh strip lights).

- While Scandi style is typically cool and clutter-free, bringing in some warmer neutral tones, or even going down to mid-toned beiges, browns and russet reds, can help things feel a little more intimate and cocooning.

'As I'm not from an interior design background I tend to unintentionally mix my styles – don't be afraid of doing the same. For example, in my own holiday home I wanted a modern Scandi-esque feel, so I went for a natural wood slatted bannister and white walls, but I also wanted a fun holiday vibe, which I achieved by adding bright pops of colour with a yellow sofa and tropical print blinds. There are no rules and if there are, the trend-setters are those who break them.'

Charlotte Fisher, Design Contestant, Series 4

NICKI'S SCANDI-SWEET TWIN ROOM

Jazzing up a predominantly white scheme with Miami-influenced shapes and ice cream sorbet colours, Nicki created a twin room in her hotel bedroom redesign (Series 1, episode 2) that felt contemporary and fresh, showing a Scandi modern influence in its use of light colours and crisp, fuss-free outlines.

The space

The use of terrazzo print on the bed linen added a graphic nod to current interiors trends (as well as to ice cream sprinkles), while the clever use of a single T-bar ceiling light - wired to enable each side to be independently turned on and off, via a matching light switch by each bed - added a simple yet playful touch. This mixture of graphic and rounded shapes provided interest, but the end result still feels relatively pared back and simple.

Get the look

+   When it comes to small spaces and designs, go for less but bigger: opting for one super-sized padded headboard across the whole bed wall looks less cluttered than two individual ones, and gives a graphic feel.

+   If you'd like to introduce a feature wallpaper but don't want it to contrast too much with the rest of the space, go for a simple design and match your painted walls to its predominant colour. The graphic black square pattern that Nicki chose above the headboard is bold, yet doesn't overpower the space due to how it blends in with its surrounding walls.

+   Try to pick up on repeat motifs in subtle ways to help your space feel united. Here, the dressing table opposite the beds was tiled with circular mosaics, and a custom radiator cover was created using circular cut-outs to pick up on this (and allow the heat to escape). Create something similar by making a radiator cabinet from 18mm ($^3/_4$ in)MDF, then use a circular saw drill bit hole cutter to add the holes.

'This look is pretty much bang on for my signature style: I love using colour on the ceiling, I love having a feature wall, I love round shapes, and I love a bit of Scandi. It's a look I'd call "contemporary urban living".'

Nicki Bamford-Bowes, Design Contestant, Series 1

boho

Bohemian style – or boho – is by nature a free-spirited aesthetic, with roots in the nomadic lives of European travellers and refugees, though today it refers more to unconventional, carefree and globally influenced decor. Its cultural roots have long been associated with artists, intellectuals and free thinkers (often with political associations, too).

Generally considered a warm aesthetic, both in terms of colours and materials, it favours a somewhat sun-bleached style, evoking weather-worn antique oriental rugs and terracotta tones. Boho style tends to borrow freely from other cultures, with influences from Eastern Europe and the Middle East remaining key to its overall aesthetic. Favouring more-is-more, boho spaces usually incorporate lots of layering and an overall eclectic look, allowing different patterns and fabrics to happily co-exist in a laid-back, harmonious way.

How to make it your own

Retro boho

- The Woodstock music festival is synonymous with retro and boho fashion trends, and the outfits worn there – crochet cropped tops, Middle Eastern-influenced kaftans, sheepskin coats and copious amounts of tassel trim – all directly influenced interiors, too.
- Rattan peacock chairs typify this look, and are also a lightweight and sustainable option. An ever-popular piece, there are plenty of new models

available to purchase, but if you look hard enough you might find an original from first time around. Pair with a round tapestry seat pad (ideally tasselled) for bonus boho points.
- Look for encaustic patterned tiles (whether the real deal or a pattern printed onto porcelain), which bridge both boho and retro looks (many tend to tread a fine line here). If you're reluctant to tile whole walls in such a bold pattern, keep it to details like a tiled coffee table top, instead.

Scandi boho

- Not all Scandi spaces are crisp white and devoid of colour: the Scandi boho trend softens the traditionally sparse looks typical of Scandi style, mixing in warmer neutrals and bringing in accents from other regions, resulting in a more worldly look which still remains relatively fuss-free.
- Popular Nordic rose-painted patterns, known as rosemåling, showcase traditional floral folk designs that date back to the 1700s and suit this style well. They mix geometric elements with flowing scrollwork art, bringing with them an air of boho-eclecticism.

- Create order by bringing in typical clean-lined Mid-century Scandi furnishings, softening them with just a little bit of boho layering for the best of both worlds.

Bougie boho

- The early '00s were awash with 'boho-chic' outfits, heavily inspired by the model Kate Moss and actor Sienna Miller. Arguably this look never really went away, but evolved into more of a 'bougie' take on boho, with moves towards glamorous, elevated details such as jewel-like drawer pulls and boho-inspired sleek geometric prints.
- Bring luxury trimmings (known as passementerie) into accent areas, such as a chic tassel dangled from a light fitting, or a detailed braid to embellish a cushion cover.
- Leopard prints give a nod to boho style, yet bring a glamorous edge: think an occasional chair clad in leopard print velvet, paired with an oriental rug.

'I'm a big fan of boho design – the idea of having no specific structure and throwing the rule book out is something I am always here for. It doesn't have to be matchy-matchy, it's the feeling you create, that spark from your personal touch and placement of furnishings.

I generally start with one object I love, be it a plant pot, a rug or a sofa, then expand from that. For me personally I like to layer textures, combine old and new, and keep everything quite pared back so you can breathe and take it in, rather than being bombarded with a ton of eclectic items plastered everywhere, which leaves nowhere for your eyes to rest, and can feel exhausting.'

Ry Elliott, Design Contestant, Series 4

'Bohemian, eclectic style is almost like you're a magpie and you've taken loads of different influences, put them in a pot, stirred it up, then created an environment out of what you get back. It's a mishmash of lots of different styles that seem like they shouldn't go together, but they do.'

Fran Lee, Design Contestant, Series 3

CASSIE'S BOHO BEDROOM

Part of a full apartment redesign (Series 1, episode 8), Cassie's clients had requested a boho-chic look. By introducing a terracotta colour scheme and lashings of texture, their previously bland bedroom was transformed into a cocooning haven, with storage hidden behind curtains and a custom bedhead complete with storage shelves.

The space

As this bedroom (located in the eaves of a Victorian warehouse conversion) already had a den-like feel, bringing this predominantly earthy tone across the ceilings and woodwork, as well as the walls, created an immersive feel. The room was also softened through the use of multiple soft and hard textures, from a bespoke timber headboard with cane weave inserts and an antique woven tapestry repurposed as a bed throw, to copper pipe wall lights and an antique dark wood washstand used as a bedside table.

Get the look

+ Revisit retro favourites such as the beaded hanging curtain, used here across a balcony door, which offers both pattern and privacy. Cassie also repurposed an old lace tablecloth into a curtain: recreate something similar by draping some vintage linen around a curtain pole or, for a no-sew curtain, source a tablecloth that's long enough to cover your window, then simply fix it to your curtain pole using curtain rings with clips.

+ Create your own boho textural wall hanging with a DIY art installation. Replicate something similar to Cassie's by attaching a metal pole to your wall using passing brackets, then hang oversized individual wool tassels from it, suspending them at different heights.

+ If your room contains exposed natural materials like wooden structural beams or bare brick walls, and you're keen to create a cosy scheme, pick out a tone from these to inform your main wall colour for a flattering end result.

+ Don't be afraid to mix pink and red tones (see pages 74-75); these two tones can work wonderfully together, but - unless you're after a very vibrant end result - stick with red as an accent.

'Cassie's introduced colour, pattern and texture to this space – it feels really cosy. It also looks timeless to me, it doesn't feel "on trend" as such, it's mixing looks that are never going to go out of style. I like the fact that she hasn't just done what she's seen in a magazine this month. It feels unique.'

Matthew Williamson, Interior Designer and Guest Judge

'There's a real confidence here – it feels like she's released her true self.'

Naomi Cleaver, Interior Designer and Guest Judge

'The homeowners asked for boho chic – I wanted to make sure I was giving them that, but I felt that to do it all with neutral colours might have ended up looking a bit dull.'

Cassie Nicholas, Design Contestant, Series 1

maximal

Generally considered to be the art of more-is-more, maximalism is often thought of as an eclectic mix of crazy clashing colours and patterns. Yet, as is often the case with complex design schemes, there's generally a lot more careful planning that goes into that effortlessly-thrown-together jumble than might first appear.

As guest judge Sophie Robinson declared in Series 2, full-out opulent glamour is a look that 'either delights or assaults the senses' (depending on your personal preferences), encompassing audacious designs and bold pattern clashes. Yet if you miss out that all-important, overriding unifying element, there runs a risk of too much becoming – well – *too much*. Even in a bold and busy scheme, it's important to retain pockets of quiet, otherwise the eye doesn't know where to go next and you can end up visually overwhelmed and possibly unable to relax.

How to make it your own

Dark exuberance

- Dark interiors can offer the chance to play with bold, busy patterns in a way that might be less intense than if you were designing in full-on technicolour. Keeping to a tighter palette of dark, subdued tones provides less visual contrast and allows you to go busier without things necessarily looking overwhelming.
- Introduce some Art Deco or Art Nouveau elements for a touch of glitz, like animal prints, mixed metals and ornamental, organic patterns.
- Bring through floral patterns inspired by the Dutch Masters, with their dark and moody still life oil paintings; this could be through an art print from the era or a vintage oil painting of this style, using that as your base to pick out the colour palette for your room; or it could be carried through in wallpaper or fabric design.

Nana's nightclub

- Coined by Series 3 contestant Banjo to describe his basement bar design in episode 8, consider merging kitsch Mid-century and retro elements with a deep jewel-hued colour palette for an interesting style mashup. Think over-dyed oriental rugs and G Plan furniture with rich emerald velvet curtains, Deco-style table lamps and Arts and Crafts-influenced wallpaper. While on paper this might sound like a visual migraine, by retaining a tight colour palette you can combine several eras together in a way that stands up.
- Bringing in textures like painted Anaglypta wallpaper gives a retro twist and offers another opportunity to add pattern in a more subtle way, filling in the

quiet spaces without overwhelming the whole look.

- Introduce luxe accents which will help bounce the light around, such as distressed copper surfaces and glazed tabletops, to stop the space feeling too dark.

Understated glamour

- Encompassing maximalism with a lower-case 'm', take influence from a maximal scheme you admire but consider how you can dial it down a little, perhaps by choosing less saturated versions of the same colours for your own space, or omitting one or two patterns for a calmer look.

- While it might sound like an oxymoron, consider trying out 'neutral maximalism' if you're not ready to go all in – think eclectic, mismatched patterns that all stick to a similar pale (or monochromatic) palette, or use another unifying design accent such as a key material. The look will be less chaotic than full maximalism, yet more interesting than a neutral scheme.

'To me, maximalism is about creating a jewel box of a room, so you feel like you're surrounded by sumptuous velvet and it's a bit padded and a bit cosy and it's rich and ripe – all those kinds of adjectives.'

Michelle Ogundehin

'If you're going to use a very bold wallpaper, which has a large repeat pattern, let it sing and let it go right up to the top of the room.'

Kit Kemp, Interior Designer and Guest Judge

'Being a maximalist is in my nature: I have always been a collector from an early age, a magpie seeking out beautiful things. But anyone can create an eclectic space – start by looking at Pinterest and interiors magazines for inspiration, get your hands on some paint chips, fabric and wallpaper samples, then start playing.'

Siobhan Murphy, Design Contestant, Series 2

LYNSEY'S DARK-LUXE DINING SPACE

Less can still be 'more-is-more', as Lynsey showed in her bold, jewel-toned restaurant space (Series 2, episode 7). This dark twist on maximalism is less about clashing designs and more about an abundance of texture, layering, rich tones and an overall feeling of warmth.

'I wanted to use rich colours and rich fabrics as well because even just looking at the space, it looked echoey. The colours of the mural have a feeling of red wine. Both mine and the downstairs space (designed by Siobhan) sit really well together – the colour scheme, the tones and that warmth really come across.'

Lynsey Ford, Design Contestant, Series 2

The space

Tasked with creating a fine dining space that reflected the local surroundings, Lynsey's busy, Dutch Masters-influenced floral velvet fabric was used to cover banquette seating backs throughout the space, providing the key colour palette that everything else was worked from. The previously echoey space felt uninviting, as well as suffering from poor acoustics, so Lynsey prioritised bringing in lots of textures - from sumptuous banquettes to thick velvet floor-to-ceiling curtains across the window wall and additional fabric partitions dotted throughout. Mismatched light fittings nod to maximalist style, though by limiting the number of different styles, and keeping them all in the same design language, the look still feels consistent.

Get the look

+ Part of creating a cocooning space is reflections; in this space, Lynsey fitted mirror glass panels across one entire wall to bounce the light around and reflect back her fabrics and colour palette. By opting for a warm tinted glass, the effect is softened. To create something similar, have some glass panels cut to size and fix them to your wall with mirror adhesive. Add mitred wooden beading around each edge, so any potentially sharp edges or corners are covered.

+ Check out online auction sites or designer fabric outlets for discontinued or end-of-line designs, especially if you need a sizeable amount. Lynsey secured an end-of-line roll large enough to reupholster the banquette seating in her restaurant for just £5.

+ Using bold patterned feature fabric doesn't mean you can't still make a statement on your walls. Lynsey chose a delicate mural design for another section of this space, in colours that tied in with the rest of the room for a calming, tonal look.

+ Painted furniture can still look glossy and high-end rather than rustic. Here, the tabletops were painted with a warm burgundy wood paint (using a roller for a flat finish); when dry, they were finished with made-to-measure toughened glass tops with a polished edge for a super-durable, wipe-clean finish. To ramp up the maximalism, you could also place wallpaper under the glass.

+ Keen to try a mural but can't find one you love? Try contacting any artists whose work you like, to see if they might be able to print one of their pieces as a mural for you (which is the approach Lynsey took).

create your own: geometric ceiling partitions

To create a more intimate feel without blocking space and light, try this wall-mounted detail (as seen in the previous page's illustration).

+ First, take two timber battens of the same length (try 100x100mm/4x4 in thickness for a sturdy frame), paint in your preferred colour, then fix to your wall and ceiling using screws and rawl plugs appropriate for your building, to create a half square.

+ Line the centre of both battens with evenly spaced nails (with sturdy heads) protruding all the way along both fronts. The more nails you add, the more intricate (and time-consuming to make) the pattern will be.

+ Take a large spool of gold twine and tie one end to the lowest nail on the vertical batten, then tie the other end to the second nail in from the wall on the ceiling batten. Cut off any loose ends.

+ Continue along the whole frame, tying your next length of twine between the second-lowest vertical nail and the third nail in from the wall. Keep going until each nail is supporting a strip of twine.

'I get such a good feeling when I walk in here – this feels really plush, luxurious and classy.'

Michelle Ogundehin

'What I love is the bravery of lots of the things she's done. She's put curtains in, and it's so right for this place, it warms it up. She's added some gorgeous smoked mirrors as well. There's something about the colours, the textures, and the lighting that leads to real anticipation, there's not a chair that I wouldn't want to sit at because my eye is going to be feasting on something. And the mural she's chosen is beautiful, it really opens the room up.'

Nisha Katona, Chef, Restauranteur and Guest Judge

Decorating by mood

meaningful influences

Trends aside, one of the key elements in a successful design is not really to do with design at all, and more to do with creating a space that feels meaningful to you – whether that's by reflecting your own cultural heritage or simply telling the story of your likes, interests, passions and journey.

It needn't be overly literal: bringing in a style you don't really associate with, or holding on to family hand-me-downs you don't necessarily like, can end up being detrimental to how happy you feel within your home. Consider all these elements alongside the importance of the feeling you're hoping to create in your room (or home), and you'll end up with a look you love that reflects both your culture and values.

'My design style is very much linked with my Brazilian heritage, but really, for me, it's more about happy memories – it's important to link your home to what makes you feel good and brings you happiness. Design for the feeling you want to create, rather than for trends. I encourage people to dig deep into their memories to find out what really connects with them and makes them smile, and that's what your home should have – your happy memories around you.

I use lots of yellow in my designs as it reminds me of the Brazilian sunshine, but when I was designing my own house I was trying to tell the story of not just my Brazilian heritage but also the beautiful walks I've had in London's Regent's Park with my children. When we moved out of London, I wanted to bring a little bit of Regent's Park with me, which inspired me to decorate with lots of florals.'

Ju De Paula, Design Contestant, Series 3

'I like to research the history of a space – design is about storytelling through colours, textures, layering and print. The brief for the cafe I designed with Banjo in episode 6 (see opposite) was "British/ Caribbean fusion", to reflect the heritage of its owners. I wanted to introduce this in a less obvious way, so I took influence from a 1940s print by the Swedish designer Josef Frank, which he designed while exiled on the Caribbean coast of Colombia. His prints are very

energetic and optimistic, which for me sums up what I think of as typically Caribbean.'

Paul Andrews, Design Contestant, Series 3

'In Malaysian and South-East Asian design, we have a lot of bare-faced red brick and concrete. Leaving walls or floors unfinished can be cost-saving, then the space can be dressed to look amazing. For that tropical vibe indoors, have potted philodendrons (in woven pot baskets) near windows that will cast gorgeous shadows against your textured wall finish.'

Karl Mok, Design Contestant, Series 4

'Art is a great way to reference your heritage, but to avoid cliches, find artists from the same cultural background or sphere as you, then use their art as a starting point in your scheme - I'm from African descent and have personally picked pieces by black artists for my own home who reference the vibrant colours and patterns typical in African design, but not in an obviously African way. They give that cultural connection almost through osmosis, then you can pick out those colours to use within your scheme to tie it all together.'

Temi Johnson, Design Contestant, Series 4

Design styles and signature styles

decorating for :
rest

It's said that our homes should be our sanctuaries, but we often need more than that. As well as providing a safe refuge, we need them to help us rest, to motivate and entertain us, inspire us, and bring us comfort. Our choice of design can play an important part in all of this.

A restful feel might be something you require from your entire home (or at least, the ability to feel rested in different rooms at different times). It can be a useful concept to get to grips with, and the answer might be to create restful corners – or removable 'busy' elements – to provide you with the perfect mix. The bedroom is a good example: whatever your preferred style, you will likely benefit from keeping the area you directly eyeball when you're lying in bed relatively serene and clutter-free, to avoid over-stimulating the eyes as you're dozing off to sleep, yet placing a busy patterned wallpaper behind your bedhead might help give you a little spring in your step when you're getting ready to leave the house in the morning.

Colours, patterns and accessories

A restful palette will generally mean one with little contrast between colours and patterns, so everything is singing a similar note. If you want to add a contrasting accent, do so sparingly, or keep it outside of key sightlines. While natural tones of blues and greens are generally the most calming, you may find a soothing pastel or even a chilled-out grey works best for you. Plants can play a pivotal role in helping us to relax, so incorporate as many as you can comfortably care for.

'I love all colours, but there always needs to be a neutral thrown in to give the room some breathing space. It is important to be bold, not frantic.'

Kit Kemp, Interior Designer and Guest Judge

PAUL'S SHEPHERD'S HUT

Although comprising a cool, subdued colour palette of sage greens, warm whites and earthy neutrals, Paul injected warmth and cosiness into his shepherd's hut design (Series 3, episode 5) with his liberal use of textures, rustic woods and reclaimed materials. His design offered a relaxing space which was easy on the eye, without any jarring accents to distract from the important activities of relaxing and enjoying the forest views outside the front door.

'I'm quite soothed by all these lovely sages and greens – this space is all about what's outside, and Paul's design mirrors that. To me, it hits the brief.'

Michelle Ogundehin

decorating for: energy

Sometimes we could all do with a little get-up-and-go, whether that's to help fire you up for a busy day at work, or to give you the energy to host a dinner party for visiting friends. Consider the key areas you might need a visual jolt, then think about how you could introduce one.

In a kitchen, this could mean opting for some bold tiles opposite your breakfast bar, or open shelves full of colourful accessories. You might even bring this into smaller details, such as ensuring your usual breakfast bowl and coffee cup are decorated with a bright, vibrant pattern. In a smaller home, think strategically about where to add these accents: simply painting the inside of your front door in a favourite bright colour could offer you a little boost every time you walk through it.

Colours, patterns and accessories

Warm, punchy colours like red, orange and yellow are perfect for social spaces and can really give you a visual pick-me-up. Busy patterns, too, can help to ramp up the visual friction, encouraging your eyes to move around the space and taking in the full design. Increase the contrast with some tonally opposite colours used as gutsy accents, like turquoise or a bold lilac. Consider creating a gallery wall filled with prints and even motivational quotes or sayings you find inspiring, for an added boost (learn more about arranging artwork on pages 238–239).

'I love how interiors are an extended expression of who you are. A cushion, paint colour and wallpaper print can say a lot about a person. In my home, it's a mix of subtle pattern and tones and then you turn the corner into another room and boom – the design slaps you in the face. That's what great interiors are to me.'

Jon Burns, Design Contestant, Series 2

PETER'S IBIZA-MEETS-THE-BAHAMAS BEDROOM

Marrying design ideas from two very different countries, Peter's bold, vibrant scheme (Series 3, episode 1) mixes Spanish influences – such as bamboo and rattan detailing in his headboard and plant pots – with a graphic tropical leaf print wallpaper, set against equally bold deep turquoise block colours reminiscent of the Caribbean. Although undoubtedly a busy choice for a bedroom, keeping the ceiling area directly above the bed white provides some (literal) light relief to ensure the overall look is not overwhelming.

'There was an awkward alcove in this room, which knocked the symmetry off-balance, so I added in a false triangular wall (by attaching wooden battens to the wall then fitting a 18mm/¾ in sheet of MDF on top, before wallpapering it) to give a more deliberately asymmetric look.'

Peter Anderson, Design Contestant, Series 3

decorating for:
cocooning

At times we all want to feel safe and cocooned, whether that's due to having had a difficult day or simply to help us unwind ready for sleep. Creating a cocooning interior goes a step beyond restful, turning a chosen room (or corner) into a fully restorative, protective space. If you're prone to suffering from stress, or identify as an introvert, carving out such a nook can be even more important for decompression.

Furniture, and its placement, can be a useful ally here: think about how you can arrange your space to create a more intimate feel away from doors, noisy areas or thoroughfares. If placement itself doesn't really help with this, choose furniture with rounded edges and curved shapes, so it feels like your sofa or chair is literally giving you a supportive hug. Protective elements such as a curved screen behind you (if your back is open to the room), or furniture with wingback sides, can also help create this cocooning feel. Bring in super-tactile materials, such as bouclé upholstery and soft area rugs, to help calm a frazzled nervous system.

Colours, patterns and accessories

To visually turn down the volume of your space, opting for darker tones and going with colour-drenching, where it's used on ceilings and woodwork as well as walls, will aid this cocoon-like feel. To stop things feeling austere, bring in natural materials like wood, and layer on lots of cosy throws to snuggle into.

'I love to use bold colours, though the tones you choose really depend on how you want your space to feel and how it needs to function for you. If you want it to feel warm, cosy and inviting, go bold with your bolds! Pick one bold colour to wrap around the whole space, perhaps even the ceiling too, to create that feeling of being hugged by colour. For a fresher, playful feel go for neutrals on walls and cheeky bold pops of colour in fun features such as bright accent cushions, artworks and window dressings, instead.'

Terian Tilston, *Design Contestant*, Series 1

SIOBHAN'S SEMI-ENCLOSED SEATING NOOK

In her holiday home makeover (Series 2, episode 8), Siobhan
opted to turn an overlooked corner into a cosy den, bringing in
a sofa and accessories which were oriented to look out onto the
striking architecture of the main dual-height entrance space. By
installing vertical wooden timber posts to semi-enclose the nook
– and visually mirroring this with her choice of striped wallpaper
behind them – she created an intimate feel which still allowed
nook-dwellers to see what was going on in the wider space. The use
of rich colours and an abundance of textiles helped the space feel
more enticing as an intimate hangout.

'This landing was a bit
of a wasted space – I
wanted to create the
illusion of a little den, to
turn it into a funky little
hangout area.'

Siobhan Murphy, Design
Contestant, Series 2

6

Sourcing and customising

'I have five Cs at the core of my aesthetic: colour, craft, comfort, character and curation.

Colour, because it is the key to happiness. Craft, because I love things that are artisanal, whether that's a ceramic pot or a lamp base. Comfort, because you have to feel comfortable in that room and never want to leave. Character, because every room tells a story: a machine can make the same thing over and over, but each object made by a craftsperson will always be different and that made-by-hand look is something to treasure. And finally, curation – because the devil is in the detail.'

Kit Kemp, Interior Designer and Guest Judge

Savvy shopping

While getting the bones and the big calls right when designing your home is fundamental, your furnishings and decor choices are make-or-break, too. Yet so often, an initial budget quickly gets eaten up by those boring but imperative behind-the-scenes jobs, like re-plastering a room because it turns out the original plaster was shot, or discovering you need a new sub-floor after removing some old laminate.

There are ways to help your budget go further once you're at the shopping and sourcing stage, however, and the first task is to work out what really matters to you emotionally (such as something you've completely set your heart on), and what must be included to make the room work for its intended function (a bed in your bedroom, for example!). From there you can form a priority list and work through the potential purchases which aren't at the top to see what you can afford.

Balancing the books

Working to a budget is often about making clever compromises and balancing needs and desires. Consider the following to help you get savvy with your shopping:

- Set your sights on a design classic piece of statement furniture? Get searching for a second-hand, as-new version; try online auction sites, local sell-or-swap pages or websites specialising in refurbished designer seconds. You could even ask your local second-hand furniture shops to let you know if they see the piece you're looking for at auctions or house clearances.

- Fallen in love with some expensive designer wallpaper? Think of ways you could maximise its impact with just one or two rolls. Would simply papering a section between a dado and picture rail, rather than skirting-to-ceiling, help you eke it out? Could you use oversized curtains to cover more of your window wall, then just paint that in a similar colour?

- Budget home-goods stores and supermarkets can be great places to snap up hidden gems, especially home accessories. Their no-frills store displays often mean that equivalent items are cheaper than you'd find in more chichi establishments, as you need to use a little more imagination to get a sense of how they might work in your own home if they're shoved on a shelf rather than beautifully merchandised in a room set.

- If you're hoping to weave in existing items alongside new purchases, remember to consider them carefully as part of your overall design picture, too.

Invest vs economise

INVEST	ECONOMISE
A great quality mattress that suits your sleep style.	A bed base - a cheap divan will function just as well as a fancy designer number, and if you cover it with a valance you won't see it anyway.
Solid hardwood furniture (a good long-term investment: simply sand out any superficial damage if it occurs, and you can also paint or stain to match evolving decor schemes).	Furniture with a veneer top (they're likely to get scratched and damaged over time and can't easily be repaired).
Window treatments: upgrading curtains and blinds with thicker fabrics and additional interlining not only cuts draughts, but it could also help reduce heating bills.	Rugs can also help keep out the chills (especially in rooms with exposed floorboards) but higher prices don't always mean better quality.

'There are excellent artificial materials which, when used in the right way, look just like the real thing – such as porcelain "marble" and artificial woods. Some vinyl wallpapers, when used in the right colour and texture, look like expensive paper-backed fabric. There are very convincing artificial leathers that can be set into desktops or used for upholstery, and I always design furniture so that the areas that can get damaged are replaceable.'

Guy Oliver, Interior Designer and Guest Judge

mixing styles and brands

In recent years interior design has steadily moved away from overly themed, matchy-matchy looks and towards a more diverse, layered style – partly due to societal changes (we tend to settle into our long-term or forever-homes much later in life than in decades past), and partly down to mass production and 'fast furniture' making it easier and more affordable than ever to regularly change the look of our homes, leading to more individualistic approaches to design.

Mixing styles isn't necessarily about a particular look – and indeed, this gently mismatched approach can be woven into a number of different styles, both purist and hybrid. Shopping around and sourcing new items from different retailers, and older pieces from across the decades, not only results in a more bespoke end result, but it also creates an interior that's easy to evolve, allowing you to swap individual items out as and when your tastes or requirements change.

There is a reason (aside from aesthetics) that the fully matching suite of furniture has remained popular for so many years, however. It undeniably makes choosing furniture easier, as the retailer has done the hard work of ensuring each piece matches across the range, giving the customer the reassurance that those dining chairs will definitely work with that table, and those sofa feet will mirror the style of the TV cabinet designed to go opposite. But by following the basic rules applied to these ranges, you can shop more broadly with confidence. Here are some key principles to consider:

- Find a unifying element, such as the undertones of the woods you use. By keeping within the same colour family, individual pieces can still feel harmonious. Oak, for example, has warm reddish undertones which work well with similarly warm-toned teak or cherry wood, while it could clash set against cool woods like ash and pine, which tend to have greyer undertones.

- Keep an eye on proportions. That matching table and chair set is created to work together, so measure carefully if you're planning to buy these pieces separately: tabletops and seat pads usually tend to sit at roughly the same heights, though these will vary across individual designs. Slowly building a collection of individual dining chairs can work out much cheaper in the long run (they tend to be a lot less valuable than pairs or sets), or mix in two or three pairs of similar styles for a look that's eclectic but not overwhelming.

- Alternatively, add an element of juxtaposition. In Series 3, episode 4, design contestants Banjo and Amy decorated their bridal shop project (seen right) in a

bold, modernist black and white colour palette, but introduced vintage elements and antique furniture to bring softness to the space, contrasting an Oriental-style rug against crisp black floorboards and repurposing an old armoire as a place to store and display accessories (which would work equally well in a bedroom).

'Your design sixth sense is all you have. Ignore Pinterest or trends – you really do know what you like. Sometimes you need to sit in a decision to know it's not right. Honour your gut – if something isn't growing on you, just change it and don't dwell (if you can't return it, save it for another room, or resell it on a marketplace site). Next time you walk into someone else's room, take a moment to stop and check in with yourself: what are you loving or loathing? How does it make you feel? What really sparks a little tingle inside you? That's your design sixth sense. Then, next time you're making a decision, wait for the tingle. That "ah-ha!" moment, a sign that yes, this is the right decision.'

Banjo Beale, Design Contestant, Series 3

shopping for vintage

Buying vintage offers even more opportunities to create this coveted layered, unique look, as well as (if you're savvy about it) save a lot of money, too. The same principles apply when it comes to combining these pieces: again, decide on the broader, overarching theme which visually unites everything, whether that's wood undertone or basic furniture shapes, or keeping any wildly juxtaposing pieces to accents (say, introducing a baroque side table into an otherwise minimalist Mid-century scheme) so it feels considered

rather than chaotic, allowing the outlier to stand out in its own right.

If you haven't really shopped for vintage before, knowing where to begin can be daunting. Going to a friendly second-hand shop or market can be a great place to start, rather than the relative anonymity of buying online, allowing you to talk to the dealers in person and get to grips (literally)

A mixture of vintage styles and eras, as seen in Jim's living room design in Series 1, episode 1

'Well-chosen pieces that are authentic and full of narrative have a profound effect on a space. Pieces with history help a space to feel as if it has evolved organically over time, rather than being pulled together all at once. Each item within a space has to earn its position there – the stories it can tell help us to connect with the space on a more profound level. Working with craftspeople on bespoke commissions excites me: their products reflect this too, and are made with passion and integrity.'

Linda Boronkay, Interior Designer and Guest Judge

'I adore using vintage, antique and preloved items in my spaces to add instant character and depth – they help create a home that feels like it's evolved over time and has a story to tell. I believe in making homes that feel more comfortable to be in.'

Tom Power, Design Contestant, Series 4

with the different styles on offer. Prices will vary depending on age, condition and the designer or make: generally speaking, vintage items (anything pre-2000) are unlikely to be as valuable as antiques (pieces over 100 years old), though that said, 'brown' furniture (traditionally styled, older dark wood pieces) is often considered less desirable than more modern Mid-century and retro finds. The former is often well crafted and eminently useable, however (and can be transformed with a lick of paint if glossy mahogany isn't your vibe), so keep an open mind.

As with other retail spaces, you're paying in part for the premises and presentation just as much as the products themselves. While a well-curated antiques store or retro shop has done a lot of the hard work for you, the best bargains are often to be found in the dustier, spit-and-sawdust salvage yards and market stalls, requiring you to have a good rummage (and a good imagination). For vintage-lovers, these treasure troves are something of an Aladdin's cave, with the thrill of the hunt offering a far bigger dopamine spike (and sense of satisfaction when you metaphorically hit gold) than a designer boutique ever could.

making things personal

Buying – whether new, second-hand, vintage or antique – is just part of the overall design picture: it's often useful to get personal, both by building bespoke things to your particular requirements and customising existing pieces so they better match your needs and aesthetic. Sometimes this is born of necessity (for example the need for storage in an awkward alcove with a sloping ceiling); other times it can be a useful approach when searches aren't yielding exactly what you are looking for, or you're keen to give your own unique stamp to something. And, frankly, it's often a lot more fun than simply buying off-the-shelf.

An introduction to upcycling

'Upcycling' can have a number of different meanings. At its core, it refers to taking a previously discarded material and using it to create something of higher quality or value (for example, weaving some scrap material otherwise destined for the bin into a decorative and useful rag rug). However, the term is now used more broadly, referring to cosmetic improvements such as painting furniture to better suit a given scheme, or using something in a different way outside of its intended purpose (like reusing an old shop display cabinet to store clothes and jewellery at home). Not only does upcycling offer a sustainable approach to home improvement, but, by taking existing items and repairing or improving them, it can also give you a great sense of satisfaction, helping you learn and improve DIY and decorating skills.

Marrying the old and new together

– If you prefer a united look, paint a motley crew of mismatched furniture in the same wood paint, to reference matching sets in a way that's still individual. This also works for blending in any new mass-produced pieces with a collection of existing vintage items.

– Has your tired old furniture got equally tired feet? Cover them with metal plinth strips (if they're straight and boxy), or use metallic contact paper for round ones. Not only can this elevate their whole look, but it's also a practical way to protect them from being bashed by shoes and vacuums.

– If you're trying to give an aged look to a new material like MDF, try painting it with several layers of moderately different colours and textures, slightly watering some layers down while painting others quite thickly using a coarse brush. Mix in a darker tinted varnish with some clear (of the same product type) to add a gently worn look.

'People often think that interior decoration is just about paint colours and window treatments, but one of my absolute favourite things to do is design bespoke items for clients' homes. I work a lot with expert craftspeople such as joiners to ensure that the finish is as good – or better – than you'd find in shop-bought pieces. But even when I make something myself, as I did on the show, I use high-end materials such as cane, marble, or interesting natural timbers. Good quality materials make a big difference.'

Nicki Bamford-Bowes, Design Contestant, Series 1

'If you do it right, upcycling can give you a bespoke, unique item that might otherwise be beyond your budget. However, there is a fine line between shabby chic and just plain shabby. If you're not confident with upcycling, choose pieces made from materials that are easy to work with, such as solid wood, then sand, prime and paint! Finish with some luxe new handles or pulls. You can also get pre-cut metal or wooden overlays, which you can cut or order to size and glue directly onto existing drawer fronts.'

Charlotte Fisher, Design Contestant, Series 4

'If you're new to decorating furniture, start with simply painting one or two different colours onto a flat-fronted rectangular piece of furniture that's not in need of repair.

I prefer not to paint antique pieces which are perfectly fine as-is (unless you know that they will end up in a skip otherwise!) so I purposefully look for pieces with scratches, stains, missing panels or other defects which make it worthy of restoration. Any signs of woodworm, whether old or new, have to be treated before you put the piece into your house, but this is easily remedied by adding wood filler into the holes – then you can paint the piece and give it new life.'

Monika Charchula, Design Contestant, Series 4

'I like to describe myself as a luxecycler, meaning I love to upcycle items but always with a luxury edge. I take the things that were on your grandma's fireplace - give them a bit of imagination, love and sparkle, and make people want them again.'

Abi Ann Davis, Design Contestant, Series 3

Creative upcycling cover-ups

You don't need to (necessarily) paint furniture as part of an upcycling project, there's a number of other ways you can cover up existing surfaces.

Putting on the glitz

Metallic leaf is a great way to bring a little razzle-dazzle into your decor, and can be used to create beautiful and varied effects. While traditionally made from real hammered gold sheets, you can now get relatively inexpensive synthetic variations in silver and copper tones, too. Sold in either square sheets or as gilding flakes, it can be adhered to lots of different solid surfaces using gold size (a specialist adhesive) before finishing with an acrylic varnish or sealer. Generally speaking, apply your size to any areas you want the leaf to adhere to (it could be the whole surface or irregular accents), leave to go tacky, then gently place your leaf over the glued areas, rubbing slowly to adhere before using a paint brush to brush off any excess. Whichever method you use should give a charmingly imperfect end result.

Try these ideas, inspired by projects from the series:

- In her show home study space (Series 1, episode 1), Cassie turned a contemporary square dark metal ceiling rose and matching art canvas into something textural yet still graphic by applying full squares of silver leaf in a slightly irregular formation, leaving slivers of dark on show as an accent.
- After an antique look? Banjo used copper leaf over an entire OSB accent wall near the entrance of his Soho bar (Series 3, episode 8) to bounce around the light and provide a visually warm welcome, as a budget-friendly alternative to real copper cladding. To complete the illusion, the wall was accented with a blend of artists paints

and glazes to create a verdigris effect, then finished with a clear matte varnish.

- Keep the gold to an accent, like Micaela did for her black-painted wardrobe doors (Series 2, episode 3 - see opposite). Brush on your size in random swooshes, then when it's tacky add your leaf (you can simply brush off the rest outside of the glued areas).

- Siobhan transformed the bar top in her restaurant design project (Series 2, episode 7), turning its original faux-wood vinyl into a glitzy serving space (which would work well on a home dining or side table, too). After applying copper leaf squares across its top, she sealed it with epoxy resin, gently pouring it over the surface and allowing it to cover the entire surface (using a foam brush can help spread it). If your tabletop doesn't have a rim, create one by adding masking tape around its edge so the resin doesn't spill over onto the floor (then remove when dry and give the edges a gentle sand).

- Apply wallpaper to the fronts (or sides) of flat-fronted furniture. Cut each piece to size in advance before carefully laying it onto its new surface. Stick it down with wallpaper paste or, for any smaller pieces, try double-sided tape (which makes it removable, too). Use a scalpel to tidy up any edges, then finish with clear matte decorator's varnish if you're concerned about durability.

- Fancy getting artistic? Add some decoupage accents by cutting out individual designs and motifs from decoupage paper (or wallpaper). Use PVA glue diluted with a little water to adhere it, then paint a few layers of PVA over the whole piece afterwards to fully secure it.

- Vinyl contact paper can be an easy way to transform furniture fronts, and offers an instantly hardwearing finish, too – as seen on Siobhan's show home console table (Series 2, episode 1), illustrated below.

Stick it up

Sometimes, sticking something directly over existing surfaces can be quicker and less messy than painting. Here are a few other ways you could transform existing surfaces with sticking:

reimagining vintage pieces

Retaining authenticity

There are no hard and fast rules to upcycling, and it can be a wonderful way to personalise pieces and also learn new DIY skills, though if you're working on older furniture, it's nice to try and include – or at least nod to – a little of its original character to retain that all-important sense of authenticity. Consider the following:

Characterful painting

- Part-paint vintage furniture, leaving aspects of its original wood finish or patina as they are, then add contrast with a splash of contemporary coloured paint. You could opt to add a vibrant tone to dining table legs to contrast with its original rustic wood top, or get creative and use masking tape and paint to produce graphic patterns across the whole piece.
- When decorating her bridal suite (Series 2, episode 3), Charlotte chose to paint a simple freehand design onto the frame of an elaborately carved antique mirror inherited with the room (see opposite); applying the paint directly and intuitively made for a quick yet striking makeover.
- Use dry brushing techniques to add subtle texture to wooden pieces: this works especially well for raised textured wood, where the paint will adhere to the raised texture only, for added contrast. As the name suggests, use an almost-dry paint brush and apply the paint very lightly to create a textured look.

New uses for older items

Use your imagination and see if you can think of ways to repurpose any existing furniture or waste materials outside of their original or intended purpose:

- As part of the office space she designed (Series 2, episode 2 - see above), Siobhan turned some old plywood cable drum reels into quirky stools, spray painting them in pastel tones first before adding a circular cushion to their tops, for comfort. To keep the cushion pad in place, secure some Velcro stick-on fabric tape to its bottom.
- A big fan of vintage textiles, when Cassie designed her hotel bedroom (Series 1, episode 2), she took some thick

fabric in a vintage Oriental-style and cut it into panels, before stapling each of them around MDF rectangles padded out with upholstery foam to create a wall-mounted headboard. To fix them to the wall so they were both flush and secure, a hidden french cleat fixing was used on each panel.

–   Make the most of the texture of old wood, like Amy did when she salvaged an old painted door to turn into a tabletop for her shepherd's hut (Series 3, episode 5). By gently sanding it with an electric sander, she removed any flaking paint while retaining the overall texture and character. Create something similar by adding metal trestle legs to the bottom of a wooden surface, attaching them to its underside with saddle clips. To make the top durable, finish in a clear matte wood varnish, or add a polished-edge acrylic sheet with rubber bumpers to its top.

tip

The same approach can be applied to smaller styling accessories, too. In Amy's retro-themed bar (Series 3, episode 8), she used old vinyl records as quirky coasters, while in Paul's beach hut (Series 2, episode 5) he glued them to the ceiling with mounting adhesive and stuck a round LED battery-operated push light in the middle, to make an alternative light fitting. Look for records that are already damaged to avoid upsetting any music buffs!

transforming the new

Antique mirror panels

*By Amy Davies, Design Contestant,
Series 3 (as seen in episode 2)*

Add a vintage aged effect to
some modern mirror tiles for
a more characterful look.

1. Set up a workspace in a
   well-ventilated, protected
   area. Wearing protective
   gloves, lay your mirror
   tiles face down on top of
   a plastic sheet, then apply a
   thick coat of paint stripper
   to their backs with a paint brush
   (follow the manufacturer's advice
   on timings).

2. Gently use a wallpaper scraper to
   remove the grey plastic backing,
   wiping away the excess paint
   stripper with kitchen roll until
   you're left with just the mirror
   layer, then rinse and dry.

3. Fill an empty spray bottle with
   one part bleach to three parts
   water, and spray as a light mist
   over the back of your mirror
   tiles, aiming primarily at
   the edges. This will erode the
   reflective areas of the mirror,
   so keep checking the view from
   the 'right' side of each tile,
   then stop when you're happy with
   the result. Again, rinse and dry.

4. Gently apply some metallic spray
   paint over the back to finish.
   This will create that warm foxed
   effect, which will show through
   in the 'bare' spots. Fix the
   tiles directly to your wall or
   background surface using removable
   Velcro pads or mounting adhesive.

PROJECT TWO

Graphic cane-panelled mirror

*By Nicki Bamford–Bowes, Design Contestant,
Series 1 (as seen in episode 1)*

Turn a simple circular mirror into a feature wall by adding a cane weave panel to visually extend it into one larger accent area.

1. Decide on your desired mirror position, then measure its width and height from the ceiling (with its centre as your guide). Measure this out onto a 18mm ($^3/_4$ in) sheet of MDF, to create a rectangle the same width as your mirror. Draw on, then cut out the top half of its circle, so your board has an arch shape at the bottom that the mirror fits into. Paint to your desired colour.

2. Cut some cane weave to the same size as your board, then attach it along both long edges of your MDF, using a staple gun. You'll need to lie it flat and weight it first so it lies straight, or alternatively soak it in a bath for 15 minutes then attach it wet (it will then become taut once dry).

3. Cut some painted wooden battens to fit along the top and sides of the MDF, mitring the corners, for a neater finish. (Secure in place with pins and wood glue.)

4. Fit your completed panel to your wall using appropriate screws and rawl plugs, so its top touches the ceiling, then hang your mirror so it fits flush into the half-circle at the bottom.

Biophilia and sustainability

With the climate crisis weighing heavy on all of us, it's imperative we consider how to make more planet-friendly and sustainable switches in our own homes, both in terms of the everyday items we use and also how – and with what – we choose to decorate them. At times this can feel like a minefield: just as with fashion, the low prices of 'fast interiors' pieces can come with hidden environmental costs, and some companies can be guilty of 'greenwashing', too, leading us to believe their wares or business model are more eco-minded than they truly are.

There are no straightforward solutions here, though a good starting point is to try, wherever possible, to decorate with naturally derived materials – from the fundamentals like flooring and furniture right down to decorations and accessories. Here are some points to consider:

Reclaimed woods

Natural wood is not only more sustainable than its faux counterparts, but studies have also shown that being around it can help nurture a feeling of calm. Seek out local sources of reclaimed wood, whether that's sheet material donated as leftovers from commercial projects, decommissioned scaffold boards, discarded pallets, or felled hardwood trees which have been salvaged and sliced into waney-edged boards. See if there are any social enterprises, council recycling initiatives or sustainability-focused timber merchants in your area.

Working with reclaimed woods needn't necessarily mean having to do all the dirty work yourself: look for a re-seller who can sand, cut and de-nail any boards for you so they're ready to use in your own home, for the best of both worlds.

Other climate-friendly choices

Choose friendly fabrics where possible. Generally speaking, anything natural and organic should come with good eco credentials, though there is an argument that second-hand or recycled synthetic material, which is already in existence, could be considered more sustainable than producing an eco-material from scratch.

Cork is a climate-positive material, meaning harvesting it has even more environmental benefits than simply leaving it in place (cork is harvested from living trees).

Cardboard packaging and postal tubes can be surprisingly durable: consider how you might use some creatively, such as for storage cubbies or even fixed around furniture bases for a cosy, curved look.

what exactly *is* 'biophilia'?

You've doubtless heard the term, but it can be bandied around quite liberally without much qualification. In essence, it refers to our innate human desire to feel connected to the natural world – and how having no tangible connection to nature can leave us feeling disconnected or even depressed. Biophilic interior design is one way to counter this, and is backed up by science. If you can decorate your home in ways that bring the outside in – whether literally, by filling them with plants and cladding the walls with natural timbers, or more gesturally, through using nature-inspired prints and colour palettes – you'll likely find this brings a sense of comfort and reassurance. Terian's bedroom design (Series 1, episode 1), shown here, offers a modern twist on biophilic design principles.

'Designing a home with nature at the heart of the process can bring that much-craved feeling of purity and calm inside, which in the long term can help our mental health, as well as being beneficial to the planet through eliminating toxic manufacturing processes.'

Peter Irvine, Design Contestant, Series 4

'Sustainability is an approach I champion fiercely. Recycled materials, antique pieces and second-hand furniture are all things that add character, history and a sense of story to interior design. We must understand where the materials we use come from and why they would fit the story of the spaces we bring them into.'

Buse Gurbuz, Design Contestant, Series 4

A nature-inspired bedroom by Terian, Series 1, episode 1

shop small

Buying handmade pieces from artisans and designer-makers is not only an easier way to get a sense of how sustainable your potential purchase really is, as you can speak directly to its maker, it also helps support small businesses and local communities, which in turn benefits the local economy. Plus, it's a great way to commission personalised or even fully bespoke pieces (which needn't necessarily mean paying more than a mass-produced equivalent).

Shopping small also offers the opportunity to buy products that relate to your region, whether that's artwork inspired by trees in a local forest, or hand-turned wooden ornaments created from locally salvaged wood. Thoughtful pieces like this, which bear the mark of their maker, can also offer a comforting sense of connection to place, in turn helping to create an interior that feels personal and connected. Here's a few ideas for ways to shop small:

- Keep an eye out in your local area for any open house art and craft events, or sign up to the mailing lists of any creative co-working spaces: many studios hold ad-hoc markets, especially around Christmas time or at the end of each season. You'll often find samples or experimental one-offs, meaning you'll get something unique which might otherwise have gone to landfill.
- Look for interesting online pop-up events which focus on bringing together communities of designer-makers:

Mindfulmarketuk.co.uk, for example, bills itself as a space where you can "shop more mindfully, consciously and responsibly" at its regular social-media-held market, while Supersecondsfestival.co.uk is a bi-annual online event where independent makers sell misprints, older stock and, yes, seconds, at reduced prices.
- Check out the websites of interior designers or stylists you follow: many are multi-talented and may have a product line or a side hustle of their own going on alongside their interiors work, selling their own art, ceramics or upcycled homewares (many of the show's design contestants have product lines which are well worth looking up - all of whom are listed at the back of this book).
- If you're not overly familiar with designers or makers in your area, look on bigger websites like Etsy and even eBay: you can filter the results by area or proximity to your home address, meaning more local makers are likely to crop up in your search results.

'I commission artists all the time to create one-of-a-kind murals, gilding, signwriting and artwork … it's often no more expensive than buying high-end wallpaper so it's always worth asking for a quote. And the beauty is that you will have something that no one else will have, something that's totally unique and personal to you.'

Siobhan Murphy, Design Contestant, Series 2

'I find nipping out and about locally to source pieces from independent retailers essential, because it gives you a unique shopping experience with someone who is proud of their business. I've found independents most useful for additional help, like how to apply the product you are buying or what's best to style alongside it.'

Jack Kinsey, Design Contestant, Series 4

'Great innovation often comes from smaller businesses, and, on a personal level, I think it's great that we have such creativity in this country, and we should be supporting it. Because of Instagram and social media, we've seen that there's a "bland-isation" of our homes that's happened with stores, coffee shops and bars, and both homes and commercial spaces are sharing much of the same look. I believe it's really important to put your own taste level in. Stuff that makes you smile in your soul, and often that comes from small designers who are creating stuff that they just love.'

Mary Portas, Retail Expert and Guest Judge

BANJO'S BOTANICAL BEDROOM

Sustainable biophilic-influenced design needn't mean serious:
in this space (Series 3 episode 2), Banjo channelled the
character of a 'drunk botanist' to create a space that combines
a strong connection to nature with a dash of Victorian saloon.

'When I create a room, I always love to create a
character, and this time I was drawn to the idea of a
drunk botanist: he's come home from an expedition in
Polynesia, he's brought some artefacts with him and
he's sitting up on his window seat, having a dram, and
life's good. This was my setting-off point. From here,
no matter where I was in the decision-making process,
I had someone to default to. What colour would a
drunk botanist's room be? A forest green, of course.
What would they use to decorate the walls? Vintage
botanical prints, naturally. And so on. This narrative not
only helps with decisions, but it also creates a fun story
for your room for friends and family to engage with,
and, really, it means you're never designing alone.'

Banjo Beale, Design Contestant, Series 3

The space

Situated in a Grade II listed building overlooking a stunning 17th-century
Italian garden, it felt pertinent to reference this important connection
through design. Painting all four walls in a bold forest green was a
literal and effective nod to the greenery outside, with vintage-style
botanical wall murals and oversized artwork offering a sense of light
relief. Quirky reclaimed elements and accessories play up to the eccentric
feel Banjo wanted to create, while opting for brown wooden antique
furniture and materials such as rattan (featured in the bedside table)
are another example of incorporating natural and sustainable materials
and pieces into the space, which further reference nature.

Get the look

+   In a featureless room, consider
ways you can add depth and
interest. In this bedroom, bespoke
joinery was added either side of
the central window, creating two
separate 'reverse alcoves', and
providing a space in the middle to
create a window seat overlooking
the garden outside.

+   Consider zoning, even in a
small space: the use of a salvaged
pub screen - which visually
separates the bed from a small
seating nook - does a similar job
to the alcoves. Mounting oversized
wall murals directly onto walls
and finishing with half-dowel wood
trim is more practical in a smaller
space than giant hung artworks,
which might get knocked.

+   Don't be afraid to go dark in a
smaller space. The warm, saturated
green here feels like an enveloping
hug - a feeling which might have
been watered down if it was only on
a feature wall, or within accents.

+   To further ramp up the drama,
add recessed uplighters to built-in
shelving to highlight a collection
of objects and create a cosy feel.

+   Introduce quirky touches:
while taxidermy might not be for
everyone, incorporating a few fun
accents that broadly work within
the scheme, but are perhaps a
little out-of-the-box thinking,
can be what takes a biophilic
scheme from overly serious to
joyfully immersive. Consider how
all the colours relate, from the
earth-toned spines of vintage
books to the choice of sunset-hued
bed throws.

+   For a full-bodied biophilic
experience, don't fake it: where
possible, stick to solid woods,
real plants and natural materials
such as linen, rattan, cork and
jute over synthetic alternatives.

create your own: upcycled bottle bedside lamp

+ Source an old glass bottle in a style and size that suits your space (at least wine bottle size is best, for stability) - try local antiques markets or your local salvage yard. Clean and dry.

+ Lay your bottle down, then place a strip of masking tape near its base (if your bottle has a decorative label, place this on the opposite side). Mark a dot on the tape - this will be where you'll drill your cable hole (the tape will stop the drill bit sliding).

+ Starting with a 4mm (0.16 in) glass drill bit, carefully drill through your mark, holding the bottle in place and going slowly. Continue with larger glass drill bits until the hole is wide enough to accommodate a cable, then remove tape and clean.

+ Using a bottle lamp kit (source online), follow the instructions for fitting and connecting the cable to the bung (which powers the bulb). Finally, add a table lamp shade of your choice to the fitting.

'It's joyful, and really smart. The room has a small window, but by framing it with the green colour and the joinery it makes it look bigger. It's beautifully conceived.'

Guy Oliver, Principal Designer/Owner at Oliver Laws Ltd and Guest Judge

'This is a small room with a small window, but what a big impact. It's a brave approach – some people would be scared of using such a dark colour for a bedroom, but it really works here; it feels cosy and inviting.'

Michelle Ogundehin

7

The finishing touches

'Creating friction is fundamental in finishing off an interiors scheme – it adds visual contrast and makes everything appear intriguing and dynamic. You can create contrast in so many different ways: through opposing shapes, or clashing textures (think smooth marble with rough wood, or hammered metal with smooth glass). Opposing elements always work, and keep a scheme from looking and feeling monotonous. Mixing materiality is something I am obsessed with: I might partner a luxurious velvet armchair with a vintage roughly hewn side table, or hang a textured waffle towel from a sleek brass wall hook. It's all about creating a multi-layered sensory space which feels interesting and compelling.'

Abigail Ahern, Interior Designer and Guest Judge

Creative effects and finishes

playing with painted walls

Paint can offer one of the most transformative ways to completely change the look of your walls, offering a lot of bang for your buck (and requiring less tools and technical know-how than papering or cladding).

When using paint to create a feature, think about its impact in the room and where best to place it, depending on where you are entering and what you are seeing first. Do you want it to literally be a backdrop, with other elements of the room acting as the star of the show, or is this your 'wow' moment? Either way, consider its overall balance within the scheme, and whether it has – or needs to have – any 'design siblings' (other design treatments or accessories to reflect or complement it).

Some simple techniques

Nervous about getting started? Try out a few super-simple ideas which are just a short step away from the norm:

- Blur your boundaries by using paint to redefine your room, instead of following its existing corners or architectural features. Paint the top two thirds of your walls the same colour as your ceiling for a cosy canopy effect, or use blocks of paint to frame key features like a statement art wall or a mirror – an effect used in Charlotte, Micaela and Peter's beauty brand office makeover (Series 2, episode 2 - see right).

- Paint on bands of colour, either using masking tape to create crisp edges or going freehand for something a little more painterly. Just as with clothing, horizontal stripes can make things look wider while vertical stripes give the illusion of taller and slimmer. Or add a bit of friction with some diagonal stripes, giving the eye somewhere to go; you could even take them up onto the ceiling, like Rochelle and Abi did in their sixth form makeovers (Series 3, episode 3).

- Line up your painted areas with other design elements in your room, such as exactly meeting the top of a console table, or aligning with a stripe in a set of curtains, to create an enveloping look (you need to be precise, so measure carefully!).

- Use low-tack sticker decal shapes to create simple patterns on your wall, such

'I like to pick out and paint woodwork in accent tones – such as architrave, skirtings, window and door frames – as these are often overlooked or painted to blend in when they can become features of the space in well-chosen colours.'

Matthew Williamson, Interior Designer and Guest Judge

as circles (as used by Paul on the exterior of his beach hut in Series 2, episode 5). Paint over, then peel them off while the paint's still wet to reveal the pattern.

Re-think the paint effect

Paint effects have evolved from their '90s heyday, after a decade or two of plain walls presiding. Try adding character and texture with one of these treatments:

- Sponging: as championed by Fran in her shepherd's hut makeover (Series 3, episode 5), her advice is to keep it contemporary by lightly loading a good quality sponge, then gradually layering up different tones of the same hue for a subtle effect.
- Go for glitz: Rochelle turned 'mould to gold' in her hotel room makeover (Series 3, episode 2), by removing and repainting her inherited mouldy walls then rubbing in small flakes of gold leaf, using size to stick it into irregular sections.
- Get rustic: use a nearly-dry brush to create an aged limewash-inspired effect with emulsion. Again, use tones in a similar palette, working with a large brush to loosely add swathes of subtle colour, working up in sections.

two ways with murals

Think you need Picasso-level artistic flair to create a feature wall mural? By following a few rules you might be surprised. You'll likely need:

+ A 2B pencil and an eraser, if you want to sketch things out.

+ Paint: water-based emulsion tester pots are a great way to amass a range of different colours inexpensively, and you can easily buy more if needed (bear in mind if you use bespoke mixes from existing leftover paints and you run out part-way through, you won't really be able to recreate that hue).

+ A selection of small and large paint brushes (a roller can be useful for larger areas, too).

+ Good quality decorator's masking tape.

how to: prep for a perfect mural

By Fran Lee, Design Contestant, Series 3

+ Create a clear plan before you start: if you're working with several different colours, plan it out systematically so you're using all of the same colours at one time.

+ Make sure you push down the edges of your tape firmly to get clean lines, and always remove when it's still wet.

+ Plan what colour you want to show when you pull the tape away: to create a different coloured dividing line, ensure your base colour is the same colour you want the lines to be, then stick down your tape and leave in place until you've finished painting.

+ When filling in any shapes, always work the paint from the outer edge to the inside, rather than painting inside to out, to minimise bleed.

+ Remember to regularly take a step back while you're working, to make sure your design feels balanced, or tape lines are straight - it's almost impossible to tell when you're close up.

+ Biodegradable wet wipes are incredibly useful to have on hand for mopping up any spills or splodges.

+ To give extra durability to your mural (useful if it's in a busy space), coat it with matte decorator's varnish once you're done.

Graphic and geometric

By Richard O'Gorman, Series 3, episode 1

+ Play with rectangular shapes by gently layering them over each other at different heights and thicknesses, in contrasting or tonal colours.

+ Turn a rectangular shape into an arch by marking out its straight vertical lines onto your wall, then draw on a dot at the mid-point between the top of the two vertical lines. Take a piece of string, tie it to a pencil, then hold its end in place over the dot so the pencil can reach the top of the vertical lines. Holding the string in place, draw a semicircle to create an arched top, then paint inside the whole shape.

+ Add in a graphic shape using masking tape to create triangles, hexagons or abstract geometrics, painting inside the gaps.

Artistic and freestyle

By Fran Lee, Series 3, episode 1

+ Decide on your design in advance, even if it's a rough idea rather than a set-in-stone template, so you've got something to copy. If you're unsure what to choose, pick out something from a pattern or shape already in the room to tie it all together.

+ For something simple, draw directly onto your wall with pencil, or mark out all the shapes with masking tape (or, if you're feeling brave, go straight in with a paint outline).

+ ' If you're recreating something more complex, mock it up first on graph paper scaled to your wall dimensions, then lightly draw the grid lines onto your walls before copying each section onto the wall in turn.

workarounds with wallpaper

Just like paint, there's no reason wallpaper can't be used in less conventional ways – think of it more as a medium, to use as part of a bespoke scheme personal to your tastes. By getting creative and adding your own custom details, twists or unusual uses to off-the-shelf papers, you can create a far more custom look on a high-street price tag.

Clever laying

- Turn your scheme upside down by wallpapering a ceiling and leaving walls plain, instead: while it's not the easiest job to do, it can create a striking look, especially on taller ceilings with ornate cornicing or ceiling roses, and helps keep your main sightlines relatively simple.
- Use several strategic strips of wallpaper to create a canopy-like effect around an area you want to feel cosy, such as a sleeping nook or sofa, as Frank did in his student bedroom redesign (Series 1, episode 4, shown opposite). Sticking with key tones from the wallpaper design across both walls and ceilings further aided this cocooning look.
- Play with the orientation of your paper: could laying it horizontally, or diagonally, create a very different overall look?

Customise it

- If your room has panelled walls, try using the inside areas of each panelled section to add a patterned wallpaper instead of paint (or incorporate this into your design if you're adding panelling).
- Bring in a decoupage-influenced, boundary-blurring effect by cutting out motifs from leftover lengths of your main wallpaper (as Amy did for her hotel room redesign in Series 3, episode 2), then sticking them to the wall instead of wallpapering fully across. Use wallpaper paste to stick them down, being careful to adhere any edges well.
- If you'd like to use more than one wallpaper design in the same space but are worried about things feeling chaotic, choose a couple of different complementary colourways from the same design, to bring a little more visual friction. Try to keep an uneven balance, as that's generally more pleasing to the eye, such as three walls in the first colour and one in the second, or even throw in one drop of a second colour among the first for a little more drama.

Frank's clever use of wallpaper helps zone this small space –
but bear in mind that a busy pattern will be the first and last things
you see on falling asleep and waking, which might not suit everyone

'Commissioning bespoke items can be costly and time consuming, so customising something like a wallpaper can be a great way to save on both those elements. For the pet shop I co-designed in Series 2, episode 4, we wanted to introduce a dog theme: I had sourced a Victorian-style eccentric wallpaper, which was just what we wanted, but the deer motifs which were in there among the dogs didn't make sense for our scheme. I decided to make it work by hanging the paper, then painting out the deer with neon spray-painted drips, which introduced an extra element of creativity and fun while giving me everything I needed from that budget wallpaper. This idea could be translated into many other designs to give your paper an extra edge.'

Charlotte Beevor, Design Contestant, Series 2

The finishing touches

alternative tiling treatments

Tiles are useful for far more than just covering walls and floors. As a strong, durable medium, available in a staggering array of colours and patterns, they are also hugely practical.

Experiment with mosaics

To create your own mosaic tiles, gather a selection of any tiles that fit in with your colour palette (try reject bins in tile stores, or ask around your local online marketplace groups to see if anyone has leftovers, as an alternative to buying new). Working outside, lay them on the ground, sandwiched between dust sheets, then use a hammer to carefully smash them through the material (ensure you're wearing safety goggles and gloves). Keep a set of tile nippers to hand, in case you need to cut

Paul's bespoke tile art offers an abstract depiction of a nearby river, and his tile colours tone into the rest of the space

any extra tiles to fit remaining awkward gaps. Stick to tiles of the same thickness unless you're happy to have some more raised than others.

tile alternatives

+   Broken china and crockery can give a quirky look, especially in a kitchen setting, though you're less likely to have perfectly flat pieces (if that's important).

+   Go for a bit of grotto-chic with a collection of shells and pebbles in place of tiles: you probably won't be able to grout these, but secure them in position with an adhesive that's appropriate for the surface you're sticking them to.

+   For a coastal nod, try tiling with sea glass: these glass fragments often wash up on beaches and have a pretty, matte, tumbled look. Start a collection until you've got enough to cover a small surface area (or take the easy route and buy some from an online crafts site).

some other simple ideas

+   Turn individual leftover tiles into coasters by sticking felt pads to their underside, so they don't damage surfaces.

+   Wrap penny tiles or small mosaics around a cylindrical vase, securing them in place with tile adhesive and grout.

+   Consider tiling any less obvious areas that might benefit from a little additional decor, like the inside of a sturdy wooden bookcase.

+   Try tiling a tabletop for added durability (or to turn an existing piece of furniture, like the top of a chest of drawers, into something more hardwearing with tiles).

+   For something a little more substantial, use mosaic tile fragments to cover a whole section of wall, like Cassie and Ju did in their reworked cafe space in Series 1, episode 6. Ensuring you have at least 30% more tiles than the area you wish to cover, start from the bottom corner, applying tile adhesive in sections as you go. Save any flat-edged tiles for the edges, then grout over the entire area once you've finished and the adhesive is dry.

how to: create a coastal-inspired tile artwork

By Paul Andrews, Design Contestant, Series 3
(as seen in episode 5 and illustrated left)

-   Take a piece of sturdy wooden board, such as 18mm (¾ in) MDF, cut to the size you'd like your finished piece to be, and arrange your tile fragments until you're happy with the overall design, using smaller shards to fill in any spaces. You might prefer to sketch a simple design onto the wood, or work intuitively to create something abstract.
-   Using a brush and some PVA glue, stick all the tiles to your back board, working one at a time so you maintain the look. Once completed, grout over the entire surface in a colour that complements your overall design, filling all the gaps (follow the manufacturer's instructions).
-   Paul's design was finished with a bespoke wooden frame, routed on its inside edge to accommodate the artwork, then screwed directly to the wall through the frame's edges. For a simpler alternative, fix on some softwood quadrant moulding around the MDF edge using wood glue, then add some mirror plate fixings to the back of your piece and attach to the wall.

wooden panelling

Wooden panelling – from simple moulding details to fully wood-covered surfaces – is a wonderful way to bring texture and character into any space, especially those that are currently lacking in it. And while different projects will require different levels of skill and expertise, there's still much that can be done at home by a newbie DIYer.

Before you go gung-ho with saws and struts, think about the type of finish you want to create: if you love rustic styles then maybe put down the ornate beaded wood trim in favour of some reclaimed wood cladding; if you like fusing together different eras, perhaps you could add a contemporary twist to traditional panelling by laying it in an unusual formation, for example.

construction notes

If you're cutting MDF panelling strips yourself you'll need a circular saw, or work out the exact batten measurements you'll need in advance and order them pre-cut. You should be able to cut any decorative mouldings with a hacksaw and mitre block. If you're working with lots of battens, you might find it quicker to use a brad nail gun alongside wood glue, allowing you to fit the entire wall before each individual glued strip is dry.

Which trim?
+ Your choice of moulding trim will influence the overall end result: straight-edged battens will look modern and graphic, intricate chair rail mouldings will nod to a more vintage style, D-shaped mouldings introduce a little visual softness, and half-moon dowels will create a playful, ribbed look.

+ Play with positioning: run battens diagonally across an entire wall for an unexpected twist, or give each individual battens a different height to create some simple graphic shapes.

+ Create more of a statement by layering up two or more trims, making each one bigger than the other, with the first sitting inside the second.

tip

Tie in panelling with other more architectural elements, such as a radiator cover or fitted furniture, to help disguise them.

tips from the trade : how to create a panelled effect

By Wayne Perrey, Carpenter at The TV Carpenter and Interior Design Masters

While exact techniques depend on what you're trying to achieve, these are the basic steps you'll need to follow:

+ Gather your equipment: you'll need a tape measure, spirit level, pencil, wood glue, knotting solution, sandpaper, a circular/mitre saw (or hacksaw and mitre block, depending on the job) and decorator's caulk.

+ Decide on your design, ensuring the gaps between your 'rails' (top and bottom horizontal battens) and 'stiles' (vertical side battens) sit evenly within the overall wall space. If you're panelling a bedhead wall, you might want to plan your design so the headboard can sit flush against the wall between the battens.

+ For a basic panelled wall (shown below left), use MDF panelling strips to create the outer frame of your panelled area first; stick down your base rail at the bottom of your wall with wood glue, then stick the top rail against your ceiling, before adding the stiles against the edge of the left- and right-hand walls. Add in the rest of your stiles evenly across the space, then add in more rails, pre-cut to fit in between each stile.

+ If you're using decorative moulding (below right), work out your plans and spacing for these, then mitre cut all your moulding trims at a 45° angle so you can place them all together like a picture frame when fixing them to the wall.

+ Once the glue has fully set, fill in the joins with caulk, allow to dry, then sand until smooth before painting with your normal wall emulsion (it's advisable to prime the untreated wood first, for a better finish - and use knotting solution where necessary).

+ Always use a spirit level to get things square and in line, but remember that many older properties are 'on the wonk', so use any architectural details (such as edges of doors or tops of skirting boards) as your main guide - your eye will always believe the architectural elements are correct, rather than a true straight line.

wood-clad walls

Cover an entire wall with wood

- Depending on your wall, and your choice of cladding, you may need to create a batten frame to attach your boards to, or you might be able to fix them directly onto your walls using nails, staples, cladding fixing clips or grab adhesive (if in doubt, ask a builder for advice).
- When cladding across a whole wall, measure up to work out in advance if you'll need to cut down your two end timbers (or top and bottom timbers, if working horizontally) to avoid one being noticeably thinner than the other, to balance these out.
- If any of your fixings go beyond a superficial level, consider potential pipes or cables that might be lurking under plasterboard (taking extra care around areas directly above plug sockets or light switches, where there are likely to be cables).

Which type of wood?

- Basic tongue-and-groove panelling is relatively inexpensive and easy to work with. Usually made from MDF, if purchasing it untreated you can paint it any colour to match your interior. Consider using side and end beads for a neat finish, and adding a dado rail on top if you're only panelling part-way up your wall (or use crown moulding with a flat top to double it up as a display ledge).
- MDF panelling strip, as used by Banjo in his holiday home makeover (Series 3, episode 7), was a budget-friendly, contemporary choice, adding a gentle detailed accent. This treatment is usually light enough to be glued directly to walls using grab adhesive.
- In contrast, Paul (Anderson's) holiday home in the same episode used reclaimed wooden panelling, which was sanded and de-nailed, to give a rustic texture (it was attached directly to the walls using a brad nailer gun). This can be more expensive, but brings lashings of character to a space.
- For a super-rustic look, use reclaimed pallet wood, selecting pieces with naturally different finishes and lengths, like Paul (Moneypenny's) downstairs cafe space (Season 2, episode 7 – see opposite).

Working with wood sheeting

Cut timber isn't the only way to bring in wood cladding – here are a few other suggestions:

- Fretwork panelling can be used as an alternative to panelled trim. Fix in place with screws, then frame it with mitred wooden beading. For something more contemporary, try using pegboard instead.

tip

Play around with the construction. As you're creating a faux wall front, could you build out your supportive battens further to create a false wall for a mock chimney breast, or incorporate some alcoves into its structure for storage, lighting or display?

- Fix plywood panels to walls for a contemporary-luxe look: for his bedroom in Series 3, episode 1, Banjo clad an alcove behind his bed with three sheets of ply, leaving a small 'shadow gap' between each panel to give an architectural edge.

- Try some simple oversized wooden shapes as a bolder wall statement by sawing gentle curved shapes into the tops of rectangular boards using a circular saw, then fixing to walls – as Fran and Amy did in their Margate cafe (Series 3, episode 6). For something smaller, take some 3-mm (⅛-in) thick MDF sheets and draw abstract shapes on them, then cut them out with a junior hacksaw and stick directly onto walls with grab adhesive – like Charlotte created in her office design in Series 2, episode 3.

If you like the look of Paul's pallet wall but don't fancy pulling pallets apart yourself, search online for already-restored pallet wood that's been de-nailed and sanded, so it's ready to use.

Ways with windows

While window dressing needs to address practical requirements first and foremost
– such as creating privacy, minimising draughts and blocking unwanted light – your
choice of window treatments can play an important part in the aesthetics of your room.

Concern	Solution
Lack of natural day light	Use a blind that sits above the window, rather than inside the recess, so it doesn't obscure any glazing when it's open.
Off-centre windows	Opt for a single extra-wide curtain that will sit on the 'empty' side, which will cover your window in one piece when needed and will balance out the space when it's open. Depending on your room layout, you could even extend your curtains across the whole wall for a generous, luxe look. Make sure you use a track or pole that doesn't require a central bracket, to accommodate this set-up.
A featureless space	Bringing in a curtain pelmet can help turn a basic window into more of a 'wow' moment. Charlotte and Siobhan championed this look across Series 2, favouring custom irregular painted MDF pelmets (Charlotte) and luxe padded designs (Siobhan). See pages 220-221 for a how-to.
Small windows	Turn them into something grander with generous floor-length curtains either side, and a curtain pole that's wide enough to ensure the curtains don't obscure any of the glazing when they're open.
Privacy	Shutters are great for adjusting the light (and views), or opt for a curtain pole system that accommodates both sheer panels (which can stay closed all day) and thicker curtains for evenings. If you prefer a fuss-free look, frosted window film is cheap and easy to apply (or remove).

After a no-sew curtain hack? Turn to iron-on hemming tape if you don't have (or can't use) a sewing machine, which turns into a glue when it's heated so you can skip the stitching. To shorten existing curtains, hang them at their intended window then, while in situ, measure how much length you want to take off. Cut off any excess length and leave just enough for your hem (around 5cm/2in is ample). Fold up this excess on the window-side of the curtain, iron flat, then place your hemming tape inside this fold. Iron again to fuse together (for ease, move your ironing board to the window and leave the curtains hanging, unless they are super short). You could also use hemming tape to jazz up a basic blind, fixing a pretty tassel trim along its bottom.

Get creative with fixtures and fittings

-   When is a curtain pole not a curtain pole? When you get imaginative! After a rustic look? Fix up a sculptural, sturdy twig to hang fixed-in-place voile panels to, or repurpose a boat oar for a coastal vibe (find one slim enough to accommodate the diameter of your curtain rings or grommets).
-   Use the same creativity when it comes to accents like curtain tiebacks or blind cleats: could an old wooden bobbin screwed to the wall work to house a blind cord, or a decorative vintage beaded necklace function as a curtain tie-back, secured on a simple hook?
-   For an eclectic look, use mismatched fabrics either side of your window (ensuring there is a similarity to their design language, so it doesn't look too random).

Wallpapering a wooden pelmet in the same design as the walls around them creates an interesting optical illusion, as seen in Charlotte's bridal suite bedroom in Series 2, episode 3

clever uses for upholstery

While there are plenty of out-of-the-box options to buy, making your own upholstered pieces can be rewarding and offers another way to create a finished look that's uniquely yours. It can also be a very sustainable aspect of an interiors scheme, allowing you to reuse existing fabric to create something new, or to upcycle a piece of furniture that might otherwise be discarded. Whatever your look, adding in some bespoke upholstery can really add the 'wow' factor and help pull a scheme together.

Get savvy with ways you can stretch your fabric budget further: bedsheets, tablecloths and unlined pre-made curtains can offer a lot of square footage for a reasonable price (more so if you shop second-hand). It can also allow you to tie a look together: buy two pairs of curtains, then hang one at the windows and use the other set to reupholster a headboard or armchair for a cohesive scheme.

'When it comes to furniture upholstery, try not to underestimate how long things are going to take, and also factor in how much working space you'll need. One of my first upholstery projects was re-covering the banquette seats in my Margate cafe makeover in episode 6: we needed to use vinyl to make it hard-wearing enough for a commercial space, but it's not a very forgiving material to work with, which made things harder. Something like velvet, or a patterned fabric, would have detracted from any creases and puckers rather than the pale pink vinyl we used, which showed every lump and bump. If you're a novice, start in the corner that will be least noticeable, so by the time you get to the front (or the more visible piece) you'll have perfected the technique somewhat. Adding on a stud trim as a style accent also gives an elevated look.'

Fran Lee, Design Contestant, Series 3

how to: create an upholstery toolkit

By Ju De Paula, Design Contestant, Series 1

I'm self-taught when it comes to upholstery, so some tools and tips that really helped me get started - as someone who needed an easy way to do things - are:

Create a basic upholstery toolkit:

+   A hot glue gun (with plenty of glue sticks) has a multitude of uses, and a fabric staple gun (with a staple remover, for removing old staples or correcting mistakes) is great for general upholstery.

+   Carpet tacks - fixed into place with a magnetic hammer - are best for creating neat corners, and help the job go faster (alongside a tack lifter).

+   Depending on the job, you may need extra items, like piping - which is useful for finishing off armchairs or smartening up cushion covers.

+   When it comes to upholstery foam, I usually use blue foam, which is thick and high density; you can also get white foam, but that's best kept to lighter-use items, like a headboard or occasional accent chair.

Insider tips:

+   When you're re-covering something - such as a vintage chair - and you're not sure how to go about it, ensure you remove the original fabric in its entirety so you can then use that as a template for your new cover.

+   Always think about ways to personalise upholstery projects: if you're just using a simple, plain fabric, it's going to look like the sort of thing you could have bought in a store, so think about how you can make it unique. I always like to use different colours and patterns within a single piece, so it's got my stamp.

+   Think about mixing different textures within a piece, as well as colour and pattern - the more textures you add, the more interesting the final piece will become and the cosier it will feel. Consider mixing linen, leather and cotton-velvet within one furniture item (or across an overall room scheme), for a really tactile end result.

three upholstery projects to try

Upholstered headboard

Based on the headboard designed by Micaela Sharp, Design Contestant, Series 2 (as seen in episode 3)

+   Re-covering an existing flat-fronted padded headboard can be a relatively easy job. First, remove it from the bed and lay it face down on the floor, on top of your fabric (the fabric needs to be large enough to comfortably wrap across the front and sides of the headboard, with a decent amount of excess material to play with).

+   Pull the fabric taut then staple to the back of the headboard, starting at the bottom, using a staple gun (manual or electric). Fold the corners of the fabric where there are any straight edges, as you would if wrapping a gift in paper, keeping the fabric taut at all times. Leave your curves until last, adding gentle pleats where necessary.

+   Finish it off by adding some cotton brush fringe upholstery trim around the edge of the headboard (securing it in place with a hot glue gun) for a luxe look.

Padded pelmet

Project by Siobhan Murphy, Design Contestant, Series 2 (as seen in episode 1)

+   Create your pelmet base from hardwood that's at least 18mm ($^3/_4$in) thick (something sturdier might be required for a large pelmet). Your

While traditional furniture reupholstery
techniques can be complex, there's plenty that
can be done on a simpler level. Try out these
three ideas from the show in your own home:

front piece needs to be comfortably
wider than your windows and curtain
pole (or track), with enough space to
accommodate the curtains either side
of the windows when they're open.

+   Cut two return pieces from the
same piece of wood, butting them
up to the front panel then screwing
together (make sure the final depth
will accommodate both your window
treatment and the pelmet's fixings).

+   For a padded look, cover it with
upholstery foam of the same size (use
spray adhesive to hold the foam in
place), then wrap some wadding around
the whole thing, stapling to the back
of the pelmet. To cover with your
chosen fabric, follow the upholstered
headboard steps. Fix the finished
pelmet to your walls with L-shaped
brackets, attached to both the short
pelmet end returns and your wall.

Hanging cushion backrest

Project by Fran Lee, Design Contestant,
Series 3 (as seen in episode 5)

+   Take a basic square cushion with
a cover of your choice, then take
two lengths of ribbon that are around
three times as long as your cushion.

+   Fold the ribbon in half, placing
the halfway fold at the bottom of
the cushion, then bring the ribbon up
over the front and back before tying
together with a knot at the top.
Keep both lengths an equal distance
from the sides of the cushion (around
5cm/2in for a standard 45cm/18in
square cushion).

+   Fix a curtain pole to your wall,
attached to passing brackets, then
suspend your cushions from this by
tying the remainder of both ribbon
lengths around the pole with a
bow. Ideally the bottom of your
cushion should be at least 5cm/2in
higher than your bed or bench seat
(depending on whether you're using
this as a headboard or chair back),
and the same from your furniture
base.

Styling and finishing touches

While it seems correct to talk about the 'finishing touches' at the end of this book, arguably it runs the risk of doing a disservice to the critical role that styling plays in making a house feel like a home, and of the power in creating a space that is curated, considered and characterful. The impact of good styling can turn an otherwise bland scheme into a showstopper simply with articulate use of accessories and artwork – though there's also a danger of relying on it too heavily, at the expense of the integrity of your design concept.

There's often a blurring between what falls under design, decoration and styling, and they can be hard to extrapolate from one another. As always, when choosing accessories, check in with your personal design needs and signature style rather than getting swayed by a shiny new thing that might be speaking a different design language or fall into the fad category (which ultimately won't bring you joy). Over-running budgets often come at the expense of styling but, where possible, try to ring-fence some money for this part of the project (shopping second-hand and upcycling will undoubtedly help here) as good styling really can give your scheme that sprinkling of fairy dust.

'If in doubt, think about how you tend to pull together an outfit – if you're dressing in all black, and everything's blended (which I like to call "stealth mode"), but you want a contrasting accent to pop out,

consider what you want to be the main focus – it could be your main item of clothing giving a "wow" factor, or your accessories. Apply the same rules when it comes to styling your home.'

Dean Powell, Design Contestant, Series 3

'When it comes to styling, first of all think of how the eye moves around the space: does it flow? Are there different points of interest? Have you used contrasting textures? Is the scale right? (If in doubt go big; there's nothing worse than a rug or painting that's too small). Next, I always like to add something quirky and unexpected as a point of interest. I tend to err on the side of maximalism - beautiful cushions, good quality candles and lamps, gorgeous artworks, rugs and plants all have a place in my design kit.'

Joanne Hardcastle, Design Contestant, Series 4

LYNSEY'S OPULENT SHOW HOME

In her living room show home design (Series 2, episode 1), Lynsey ramped up the glamour in her dark, cocooning design using gold accents to unite the whole space; this warm accent graced wall cladding and furniture, right down to artwork and accessories. The look was tempered with plenty of grounding greys and luxe textures.

'There's an enormous amount of design bang for your buck in here... I really like the vertical slats of wood on the wall that blend into the curtains; it's very playful, quite surreal, but also very sophisticated.'

Laurence Llewelyn–Bowen, Interior Designer and Guest Judge

'shelfies' and display spaces

While it might seem like a dark art, there are actually basic rules and principles you can follow to create a pleasingly styled composition (and, of course, once you're familiar with the rules, you can always choose to break them!). When it comes to the shapes and configurations our eyes find pleasing, this often relates back to nature: artists have long found that the 'rule of thirds' can make for the most visually pleasing compositions when painting sea or landscapes, and the same applies to physical ornaments, too.

Key styling principles

- Stick to odd numbers, such as three or five objects grouped together, rather than two or four (though you could arrange your five as three on one side, two on the other, as part of this principle). Keeping things asymmetric and varied, while retaining some empty space around them, gives the eye more to do, which makes it more interesting to look at.
- Play with differing shapes and heights within your groupings, but keep a shared element of design language, such as colour or material.
- Try arranging grouped objects so they overlap slightly, allowing them to read as one entire arrangement. You can also ground smaller, bitty pieces by placing them on a tray, or stand them in front of a leaning artwork.
- If you *do* want to create a symmetrical look, make sure that it's perfectly aligned, so it has the desired effect (if things aren't either perfectly aligned or clearly purposely asymmetric, it can make everything look unbalanced).
- To avoid style over substance, mix in the odd quirky, vintage, spectacular or personal element; and if you truly love something, absolutely include it – it'll make you happier than any generic matching vase ever could.

tip

Check out your compositions by looking at the space through the camera function of your smartphone, with the grid lines switched on: is your vignette balanced? The illustration opposite, showing a styled console top designed by Abi Ann Davis (Series 3, episode 1) demonstrates many of these rules in action.

'When I worked in merchandising,
I often visualised the retail spaces I
styled as like being inside a pinball
machine: when the ball is released,
it pings off various different random
points, and when you walk into a
room, your eyes will naturally do a
similar thing to that pinball, darting
around and reacting to various
different places they hit.

   To bring the drama of that
proverbial pinging pinball into your
home, you need both high and low
points: some accents (those pinball
moments) to give little pockets of
drama – but also those passing
places, so your eye has somewhere
to rest. Whether it's designing a
commercial space or your own
home, the principles are the same.'

Paul Andrews, *Design Contestant, Series 3*

'Styling is one of my favourite things
to do – I view it as a little treat at
the end after all the hard work of
designing and installing a scheme.
I tend to work on one vignette
at a time, whether that's a set of
shelves, a coffee table or sideboard.
I add all the big objects in first, like
lamps or large plants, then layer in
smaller items, being careful to use
different heights, materials and
textures. Books are great to style
with: I like to stack them up, adding
a plant or vase on top. Flowers are
also brilliant for adding colour and
softness to your space, especially
if you are styling with a lot of hard
materials such as metal and glass.'

Siobhan Murphy, *Design Contestant, Series 2*

styling (or hiding) your tech

Our homes are increasingly tech-filled these days – with TV screens, speakers, smart home hubs and endless cables – and while the designs of these items have both improved aesthetically and shrunk physically over the years, they can still be a bane when it comes to styling your space.

Cable management

Nothing lets a look down quite like a sea of tangled, unruly cables, so where possible consider ways to hide them that still leaves them accessible when needed. This is generally easy to do behind solid-backed furniture, but for furniture like console tables, work them down the back legs using stick-on cable clamps, helping to secure them out of sight. For cables that don't ever really need unplugging, gather them together into one bundle (you can buy cable tidy tubes, or, for a softer look, try tying them together with twine) then hook the whole thing somewhere incongruous. Cable trunking is also a good way to lessen their appearance: paint any plastic piping the same colour as your walls or, for an industrial look, make a statement with steel trunking.

Cosy it up

By default, tech is usually shiny and plastic, which can look somewhat other-worldly, especially in more rustic and vintage schemes. Think about ways to hide items, while still keeping them accessible, by customising other types of containers to store them in. Take that ugly paper shredder; would it work in a lidded rattan storage box, if you cut a little space in the back for its electric cable to pass through? Internet routers can be tricky as they generally need to be left uncovered, but could you place a few books or a picture frame in front of it, so it's visually obscured somewhat? And while we'd all love to say otherwise, in reality we all have a bunch of random plugs and cables just knocking about: set up a pretty lidded storage basket to house them all in, at least until that rainy

tip

There is of course tech that helps us to manage our tech now: items like phone charging pads, and plugs with USB ports, can all help minimise electrical clutter.

day when you actually sit down and work out what they are all for...

Transform your TV

-   Fake a focal point: if your room doesn't already have a chimney breast, add a false wood-panelled one to a wooden frame, incorporating an inbuilt recess for your TV, like Kyle did in Series 1, episode 5. While it can feel unsympathetic to place a flat-screen above an ornate Victorian fireplace, it's arguably a little more in-keeping as part of a modern design.

-   Hide your TV in plain sight by standing or hanging it in front of a dark wall, so it visually vanishes when switched off. Placing it off-centre and surrounding it with a black-framed gallery wall will equally help disguise it, allowing it to get lost in the midst.

-   Consider any clever cover-ups – such as a bespoke roller blind hung above a wall-mounted TV, designed to look like an artwork or tapestry when it's pulled down (you may need to fit a wooden batten above the screen to attach the blind's brackets to, so it has clearance). This technique was used by Molly for her hotel bedroom design in Series 3, episode 2 (see above), and created using a DIY roller blind kit, which she fitted with her own bespoke canvas design, though an off-the-shelf blind would equally do the job. If budget allows, an electric roller blind can automate the transition.

-   While old wooden TV cabinets were designed for far boxier TVs than we commonly have these days, they still have a vintage charm: look out for any designs that might accommodate your modern flat-screen, ideally with doors so you can shut it away when not needed.

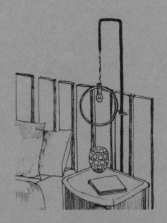

Shadow-box light panel

Project by Nicki Bamford-Bowes and Frank Newbold, Design Contestants, Series 1 (as seen in episode 6)

+   Fix a frame to your walls with 5x5cm (2x2in) timber batten, leaving a short gap in either the bottom left or right corner to run your lighting cable out from. Fit two plug-in LED strip lights inside the top and bottom battens ensuring they sit fully within that recess (make sure they are switched to 'on', so you can manually turn them on and off at your external plug socket).

+   Gather together some oversized faux plant leaves then attach them across the wall in between the battens, fixing them by their stalks using cable clips (make sure they are a safe distance from the strip lights).

+   Screw a sheet of frosted acrylic sheet, cut to size and with polished edges, across the battens (if their sides are visible, you could paint them to tie in with your walls).

Elevated bedside lamps

Project by Lynsey Ford, Design Contestant, Series 2 (as seen in episode 3)

+   Source a decorative hanging plug-in bulb and shade set on a vintage-style braided flex. Unscrew the plug socket and set aside.

+   Take a length of copper pipe plus an L pipe of the same width and use epoxy glue on the inside of the joint, to secure them together. It needs to be tall enough to travel upwards from the top of your skirting board to taller than the height of your headboard, then protrude outwards to roughly where the centre of your bedside table sits. Fix the pipe in place using munsen rings (if you'd prefer a different colour than copper, spray paint it before fixing).

+   Thread your lighting flex through the pipe, and adjust the light so it hangs at your preferred height by supporting the cable at the bottom of the pipe with a cable clip. Re-attach the plug.

lighting & lamp hacks

Styling up your own light fittings can give you a bespoke effect on a thrifty budget. Have a go at the following hacks, to whet your appetite.

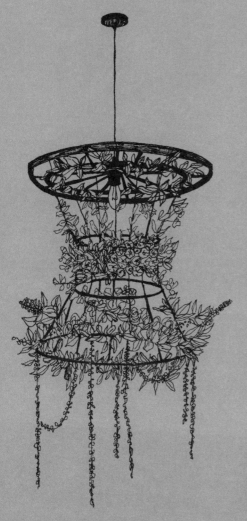

Upcycled faux floral shade

Project by Amy Davies, Design Contestant, Series 3 (as seen in episode 7)

+   Take two existing wire-framed lampshades, strip off the fabric, then spray paint the frames in a colour of your choice (these will be visible). Fix them both together with clear cable ties to create one large fitting, with the first shade's bulb fixing still at the top.

+   Begin winding a selection of faux flowers and foliage horizontally around the fitting, weaving them through the shade's frame, securing as you go with smaller cable ties. When you're happy with the look, and if ceiling height permits, weave in some extras along the bottom and allow them to hang down for added drama.

+   Fix to your existing ceiling pendant light fitting, ensuring the shade and flowers sit well clear of your bulb (if you're concerned, you could spray the faux flowers with a fire-retardant spray before hanging).

soft-scaping

While technically a term used to refer to the softer, planted elements of garden design, it works equally well when applied to interiors: without those tactile touches of cushions, throws, curtains and rugs, our homes would feel harsher and unwelcoming.

These softer elements can be deployed even in typically 'hard' spaces like kitchens and bathrooms through the use of linen hand towels or fluffy bathmats, regardless of your style or scheme: even a minimalist space will benefit from a softer touch. However, as always, beware of adding design for design's sake, and check in to see if your soft-scapes are bringing something necessary, useful and relevant to your design, or simply ticking off the texture-box.

To chop or not to chop?

While some designers feel that anything other than a crisp, karate-chopped cushion configuration looks untidy (this is where a cushion's top is indented by hand to give a 'chopped' centre and raised 'ears', as seen in Paul's pristine show home design in Series 2, episode 1 (shown here), for others it gives a far too formal feel. Neither is wrong, but consider which is more you: if you're creating a country-boho scheme, then perfectly configured boutique-hotel style cushions might throw the whole thing off (and vice versa). Generally speaking, the same styling rules apply to cushions as to ornaments: if you want it sleek and symmetrical, keep it exact, otherwise aim

for groups of odd numbers and bring in a few different sizes and formats, layering any smaller circular or rectangular cushions on top of larger square formats.

Get creative with repurposing

-   Who says rugs are only for floors? In Amy's retro bar space (Series 3, episode 8), she hung a circular shag-pile rug to the wall to create a graphic yet textural alternative to art: fix similar in place with some panel pins or screws, depending on weight. Alternatively, suspend a patterned flat-woven rectangular rug on your wall from a pole on brackets (add some fabric loops to its top or side to hang it from).
-   Change up the look of a cushion cover by creating a 'sleeve' for it: choose some fabric that's slightly shorter than your cushion pad, wrap it across so the two pieces meet up at the back, then place some iron-on hemming tape between the two fabric layers, running an iron over it to form a bond.
-   Large rugs can be expensive: for a boho look, copy Banjo's tip from his 'Nana's nightclub' bar space (Series 3, episode 8), where he fixed several smaller short-pile rugs together using carpet tape on their

underside. Or, for areas where it won't cause a trip hazard, simply layer on a few different rugs, allowing them to overlap. Getting carpet whipped (where the edges are neatened and reinforced with stitching) can also be more cost-effective than buying a super-sized rug: visit your local carpet showroom to source cheap offcuts, and ask them to whip the edges for you.

- Try placing a chunky throw (or even a flat-weave rug) across a sofa back, to add in a new pattern and texture and also offer protection from wear-and-tear.

outdoor living

The trend for outdoor living – treating your garden, yard or balcony spaces like an extension of your home – is continuing to blossom (if you'll pardon the pun), as we collectively move towards designing our al fresco spaces with as much care and attention as we give our interiors. Creating an outdoor space that reflects your signature style and offers multiple uses can be both fun and rewarding, but it's important to keep practicality and durability in mind, to minimise any costly (and wasteful) deterioration of furniture and accessories.

Keep the pretty practical

- Where possible, ensure any wood you use outside is pressure treated (a chemical treatment it undergoes to ensure it will last outside for far longer). If you've inherited existing wooden furniture or decking, treat it with a protective exterior wood paint or oil to enhance longevity.
- While there's an inherent charm (and good sustainability credentials) to natural rattan outdoor furnishings, if you're unable to store inside over winter (and cover on wet days) it will likely perish quickly. Arguably, if you need to leave pieces outside year-round, a PE synthetic rattan can be your best bet, and can also be recycled at its end-life.
- Similarly, weather-proof polypropylene woven rugs can be left down all year and simply hosed clean as required. Look for designs made from recycled plastics, such as drinking straws, over virgin plastic.
- Outdoor textiles have traditionally been pretty basic, though increasingly you can find a wide range of designs which are indistinguishable from their interior counterparts (usually made from synthetic materials like polyester or olefin). For a bespoke look, source your own outdoor fabrics and some compressed fibre cushion pads and create your own set.
- Keen to re-cover some existing outdoor sofas? Try using waterproof awning fabric for a bold look (and durable finish).
- Turn an outdoor table into something more decorative by tiling its top (see pages 210–211 for details). Ensure your tabletop is flat, solid and suitable for outdoor use before tiling, and use frost-resistant tiles.

Smaller spaces

- If you've got limited square footage, go up instead, making the most of walls and fences by adding vertical planters. You can buy ready-made kits, or simply make your own by fixing some horizontal railings to your upright surface, then suspending hanging plant pots from them.
- Find a modular L-shaped sofa that's tall enough to also double as banquette seating for an outdoor dining table if you

zone off a garden space

Pagodas can be a great way to add both shade and privacy to an overlooked outside space. On the decking area of her chalet redesign in Series 1, episode 5, Cassie opted to create a free-standing pagoda (see below) to get around the issue of not being able to fix anything permanently into the ground. By creating four tall rectangular planters from pressure-treated decking boards (see over the page for instructions), then securing pressure-treated square battens into their corners to form part of a simple pagoda frame, this provided a cosy spot to dress with a padded bench seat, table and outdoor accessories. Adding climbing vines inside each planter means that over time they will cover the entire structure. The space was finished off with solar-powered festoon lights, offering pretty and practical evening illumination.

Cassie's pagoda on the decking of her holiday chalet re-design works for both daytime lounging and evening entertaining

don't have space for separate lounging and dining areas (generally, your seat should be around 45cm/18in from the ground to work with a standard 70cm/28in tabletop).

– Only got a small balcony with no space for a table? Add on a wooden ledge, like Amy did on the decking of her holiday home design (Series 3, episode 7). Crafted from a scaffold plank, it was custom fitted to the space. Get the look at home by fitting a purpose-designed railing shelf kit, then slot a couple of bar stools underneath.

choosing and customising plants and pots

Growing houseplants can be addictive and very rewarding, helping enhance your connection to nature as well as adding texture and softness to your space.

Which plants to choose?

The same aesthetic rules apply to plant styling as any other ornament or accessory (see pages 224–225), such as working with odd numbers and playing with size, shape and scale, though of course as living things, you may need to move them around to find the spot that suits them best.

- After a boho look? Desert plants (think cacti and succulents) will work well for this (and they're pretty neglect-proof, too, so can be good for a new plant parent).
- Maximalist schemes work well with equally busy specimens: try ferns, or opt for something with bold patterned leaves like the polka dot begonia, or alternatively a bright, showy orchid.
- Prefer something more structured and architectural? Go for a plant with simpler shapes, such as an aloe, fishbone cactus or a string of hearts.
- Enjoy immersive, 'urban jungle' vibes, with plants suspended from every surface? Build up slowly to see what suits your space, but once you get going, go for broke and utilise ceilings for trailing specimens, floors for oversized indoor trees and any other surface in between for whatever else takes your fancy.

Plant pot hacks and displays

- Create a display space for hanging planters above a kitchen island or dining table: take some wire mesh and suspend from your ceiling on chains attached to cup hooks (try to locate a joist to screw these into, for support). Then hook any hanging planters directly from it.
- No budget for decorative planters? If your plants are happy for now in their plastic grow pots, simply disguise these instead: spray paint them in a vibrant colour, pin a fabric offcut around them, or slip over a kraft paper sleeve.
- Get loose with the term 'plant pot': depending on your plant size you

tip

Real is always preferable to faux, but in specific spaces – such as a windowless bathroom – fake plants are arguably a more practical choice than bringing in real plants, which wouldn't survive long in that environment.

'Plant or flower walls not only look beautiful, but they also transform the whole feel of a room. For practical reasons, I used faux for the flower wall I designed for my lingerie shop scheme in episode 4: I created a simple trellis system using pond mesh stapled around a wooden pallet collar (essentially a rectangular frame), which was screwed into the wall. The flowers were then threaded through the mesh and secured with staples and cable ties. For a domestic space, I'd have used real flowering plants in a planter base underneath the trellis system, then trained them to grow upwards using cable ties and string.'

Molly Coath, Design Contestant, Series 3

Molly's lingerie shop scheme, Series 3, episode 4

could pot it up in a vintage jelly mould, decorative tin or old wooden barrel. If there's no option to add a drainage hole, line its base with gravel before planting.

Make a DIY wooden planter

-   Take four pressure-treated decking offcuts, cutting two pairs of two at the same length.
-   Drill through the front corners of one length of wood, attaching it to the side of your second piece to create a butt joint. Repeat at the other end, then on the other side, to create a square or rectangular grid.
-   Screw more wood panels across the base until you have an open-topped box, then drill in some additional holes for drainage. Staple a black membrane to the inside, then paint with an exterior wood paint or leave au naturel. You could make square planters with additional wooden feet (like Paul and Banjo created for their cafe redesign in Series 3, episode 6) or opt for a long, skinny tabletop planter similar to Charlotte's in Series 2, episode 2.

The finishing touches

clutter-busting and storage solutions

Although a less sexy topic than styling, storage is equally as important as any curated displays: whatever your overall look, most homes will need a mixture of both. It's easy to get caught up in fanciful aesthetics when designing a space and inadvertently overlooking the everyday detritus of life, but failing to accommodate this risks letting down your whole scheme.

Generally speaking, small storage solutions tend to fall into one of two categories: use it (incorporate either the items you wish to store, or the vessels to store them in, as part of your overall design scheme) or lose it (hide it all away, for a more seamless look).

Use it

- Decant kitchen and bathroom goods into glass storage containers or vintage bottles (large, used jam jars can be a great way to cut costs here, to supplement a set of Kilner jars). If you need to label these with product types or best-before dates, write directly onto their fronts with a liquid chalk pen, or use chalkboard stickers.
- Pretty vintage cake tins can be used for holding smaller items, foodstuffs or even as a fancy receptacle for your pet's favourite treats.
- Basket bags on the backs of doors can be handy for assigning specific storage duties to - such as children's toys, to get them off the floor - or use them more practically as a temporary catch-all for stuff that's in the wrong room, then at the end of the day you can carry it with you and re-home everything correctly.

Lose it

- Clad an entire storage cupboard and its surrounding wall in wooden panelling so you can barely tell it's there (a technique successfully used by Lynsey in her holiday home bedroom in Series 2, episode 8). Alternatively, try wallpapering flat cupboard doors and fit them with a push latch mechanism, so their functionality almost disappears from view.
- Use a vintage chest, crate or ottoman in place of a coffee or side table. It won't take up any more floorspace, but could hide a multitude of sins inside it.
- Consider constructing freestanding furniture which contains 'secret' storage, like the Crittall-inspired floor-length mirror designed for Banjo and Amy's bridal boutique makeover (Series 3, episode 4, see opposite). While this was bespoke made from MDF, you could create something similar by repurposing two slim bookcases: place them back-to-back and join them together using strong construction adhesive, then place its now-back against your wall, so you can access the shelving cubbies from either side. To create the Crittall glazing effect, source

some self-adhesive square mirror tiles (enough to cover what's now the 'front'), then use some slim strips of wooden beading (pre-painted black) to cover the joins between each tile and finish off the edges, securing them with more construction adhesive. You may need to cut some of the glass tiles to fit the back (which can be done with a glass cutting tool) or, alternatively, order pre-cut glass squares to fit the space exactly.

tip

Some designers advocate the 2:8 principle, which refers to the concept of keeping 80% of your belongings put away with 20% out on display. Other designers advise allocating at least 10-20% of each room to storage. When factoring this in, keep in mind both your signature style and preferred visual friction levels: for some, a very streamlined space is the dream, whereas for others it could feel bare and oppressive.

Using art

choosing and arranging

A home with bare walls is a bit like an outfit with no jewellery or accessories: yes, it's probably perfectly fine as it is, but ultimately it's likely to feel unfinished, or a little flat. Arguably, your choice of prints, paintings and wall hangings offers one of the best ways to truly reflect your personal style. Though if you're starting from scratch, working out what to put on your empty walls can feel as daunting as an artist might find staring at a blank canvas. Luckily, there are plenty of frameworks to follow.

Find your style

While Instagram is awash with cool, curated (but sometimes samey) gallery walls, try to tap into the styles you truly love rather than getting caught up in trying to choose things that perfectly co-ordinate with the rest of your decor. Consider, too, how you want the finished look to feel – are you after a calming, relaxed vibe, or looking to make an eye-catching statement? This will all impact the styles, colours and subjects you choose.

How to hang

Arranging

Our brains are said to favour looking at artwork with its centre roughly level with our own eyeline, which is generally agreed to be around 145cm/57 in from the floor (for a gallery wall of multiple prints, aim for that central height to be at the mid-point of the overall arrangement). Though if you're hanging pieces over statement

furniture like a sofa or headboard, you may want to bring this down a little, to create a more intimate feel.

To stop a wall of multiple prints feeling disparate, you need to choose which 'rule' to follow in order to create a sense of consistency. For a gallery wall, this could mean lining up all your pieces to create a box shape (where the outer edges of the pictures line up to form a square or rectangle – see bottom example opposite), or keeping a fluid outer outline but bringing in consistency to the gaps between each individual artwork (as the top sketch shows). Or you could choose a common design element to create order – sticking to all-black frames, for example, or a particular colour palette within the artwork.

Fixing

How you fix pieces to your walls will depend on their weight: lighter frames and canvases can usually be hung on a single

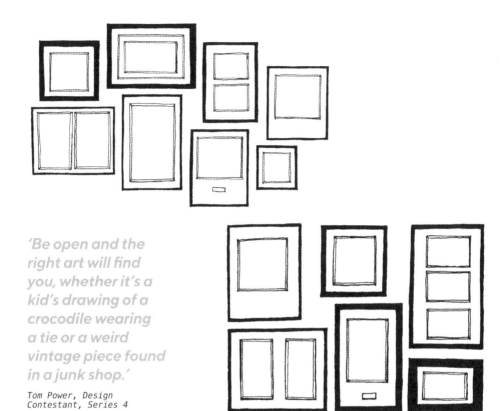

'Be open and the right art will find you, whether it's a kid's drawing of a crocodile wearing a tie or a weird vintage piece found in a junk shop.'

Tom Power, Design
Contestant, Series 4

or multi-pin picture hook, while heavier pieces with large glass (instead of lighter acrylic) glazing will probably need to be hung from a protruding screw secured with a rawl plug, or even fixed to the wall directly using mirror plates. If you're reluctant to make lots of holes in your walls, search for picture hanging strips, which come in a range of strengths suitable for different frame or canvas weights (and they don't damage walls, so are a great option for renters). Alternatively, fix up a picture ledge, which allows you to lean and rearrange a selection of pieces on its surface, or even reinstate a picture rail, which you can suspend artwork from on moulding hooks to minimise wall damage.

Adding interest

Incorporating non-art pieces helps bring friction and depth to a gallery wall. Frame up some favourite paper packaging, pop in a pretty plate (secured on a plate hanger), or tack up a decorative bookmark in an awkward gap, for a less formal feel. Alternatively, look into other non-art items you could hang: in Nicki's show home bedroom design in Series 1, episode 1, she suspended a vintage kimono from a wall-hung pole, while Siobhan's hotel bedroom design in Series 2, episode 3 featured an oversized vintage fan fixed directly to the wall.

The finishing touches

DIY projects to try

Whether you think you are or not, we all have the capability to be creative and make beautiful things. Designing your own decorative wall art is no exception, and needn't require any specialist skills or abilities, just an open mind (and a few strategic tools, of course). Here are some ideas inspired by the show:

Simple projects

- Got an offcut of pretty fabric (or maybe even a vintage scarf)? Pop it in a picture frame instead of an art print, as Lynsey did in Series 3 episode 8.
- Try cutting interesting shapes from leftover decorative flat materials to add texture or pattern to otherwise featureless walls. Frank, for example, mirrored design elements used elsewhere in his student bedroom redesign (Series 1, episode 4) by fixing triangular OSB accents to a wall with construction adhesive.
- Fix some 3D wall-panelling tiles directly to your walls with construction adhesive; arrange several together for a unique effect, like Charlotte did in her show home bedroom in Series 2, episode 1.

Get hands-on

- Resin is a wonderful medium for making creative wall hangings: Amy used some to preserve pressed flowers as part of a hanging sign for her shepherd's hut project (Series 3, episode 5). Mix epoxy and hardener (follow the manufacturer's instructions) to form the resin, pour it into a silicone mould and layer in your pressed flowers. Once dry, remove, then drill holes into the corners to fix it to your wall.
- Create your own canvas artwork, a technique used several times by Molly in Series 3. Create a sketch and scan it into your computer (or draw it directly onto a tablet, using a drawing app and digital pen), then save your finished design as a JPG file. Search online for a local print shop to print it directly onto a loose or framed canvas (see also page 112 for advice on creating your own repeat pattern).
- Make bold, graphic art shapes, as Terian did in Series 1, episode 1. Take several vinyl sheets in complementary colours, then cut them into different bold shapes

Amy selected the flowers used in her hanging sign from the
locale of the area it now hangs in

using a scalpel. Peel and stick onto a card background which fits your frame, layering them to make bespoke patterns.

Spell it out

Typography artwork remains ever popular, and can be a great way to bring a personally meaningful slogan into your scheme. Try these ideas:

- For a retro look, source some dry transfer lettering. Following the instructions, rub it onto a decorative paper background (such as a patterned wrapping paper sheet) to form a word or phrase. In Barbara and Lynsey's camera shop makeover (Series 2, episode 4), shown over the page, they applied their text to sections from a vintage map, secured in a frame.

- In his Soho bar redesign (Series 3, episode 8), Banjo transformed an existing freestanding mirror by adding the welcoming greeting 'you look like you need a drink' in Victorian-style signwriting to its surface (see left). Create something similar with liquid chalk pens. Sketch it out first, then use masking tape to create guidelines on the mirror's surface before drawing directly on it (you can remove any mistakes with a damp cloth).

- Use cable or decorative cord to create 3D words directly onto your wall (Siobhan created the word 'wireless' in the office space she co-designed in Series 2, episode 2). Draw out your design on paper and copy onto your wall in pencil, then use panel pins or cable clips (depending on the thickness of your cable or cord) to secure it into place and make the correct shapes.

The finishing touches

What next?

Making it personal

By now, you should have a clearer idea on how you can create an interior that not only looks great but, most importantly, reflects your personality. And, hopefully, you're now feeling inspired to try out a previously planned project, but also pumped to experiment with ideas you hadn't considered in the past.

Perhaps above all, you're feeling like this could be fun rather than something to find daunting. Yes, renovating can be stressful (especially works that are particularly disruptive or messy), but where possible lean into the process, remain open and honour your gut – being brave enough to make more daring choices, yet listening to your intuition if something just isn't feeling right. Also remember that knowing when to hold back and show restraint can be just as brave as going with bold, clashing colours and prints. Unlike in the series that has inspired this book, you're *not* in a design contest and there's no one judging you at the end (other than possibly yourself), so really put the work into creating something that honours your feelings, heritage, family and environment. Stick with what you truly love, and you can't go far wrong.

Some final words of inspiration

'Capturing the senses in our homes is even more important now, as we have realised how vital our homes are to us as places of refuge, places of connectivity, places of family and of creativity.'

Mary Portas, Retail Expert and Guest Judge

'Treat your home like its the museum of you, displaying the history and adventures of its owners. To create a personal and unique home all you have to do is fill it with objects that have meaning to you, such as photographs, souvenirs and art that you connect with, and it becomes part of your history.'

Monika Charchula, Design Contestant, Series 4

'It's sometimes hard to find and define a style of your own – I've learnt not to follow the crowd and I don't fit into particular box or genre; I've found a place somewhere between eclectic glamour and dark decor which

Barbara and Lynsey injected personality into this previously bland space (Series 2, episode 4) with custom seating, cheery yellow tones and bespoke artwork

I find suits me well. I'm such an avid collector and love to mix up different styles. Vintage is a passion of mine and I find such a thrill in hunting down the perfect treasure to finish off my scheme. I choose things to display around my home because I genuinely love them, not just because they fit with a theme. If you stay true to what you love and what excites you, your own style will always shine through'

Joanne Hardcastle, Design Contestant, Series 4

'Interior design should be fun. There are a million and one ways to design a space, and so many decisions to be made. Invariably, you'll get things wrong, but that's where the magic happens and you stumble across something magical, like an unexpected colour combination. Remember, a space never has to be finished, it's evolving. Go easy on yourself and enjoy the ride. Buy pieces that you love, that make you feel something. Avoid big box stores and fire up an online marketplace in a completely new city. Make a day of it and go collecting treasure in a new place – you'll have fun and meet some amazing characters, see new sights and pick up treasure you would never have found in the specials bin at your local warehouse store.'

Banjo Beale, Design Contestant, Series 3

The finishing touches

how to become a professional interior designer

Has this book got you hankering to change careers, as many of the contestants across *Interior Design Masters* have done, and become a professional interior designer? While there's a range of courses online teaching you how, from one-off webinars to full diplomas and degrees, you could equally build up from budding amateur to professional status using any pathway that works for you and your timescale/budget. Here are some words of wisdom from the design contestants to inspire you:

'Fake it 'til you make it! Start creating mood boards and schemes for imaginary clients. Set yourself imaginary briefs, then share these designs on social media and with anyone you can. This way you will learn, grow and develop your own design style, and then your people will come to you!'

Molly Coath, Design Contestant, Series 3

'One of the best things about being an interior designer is that you can branch out the services you offer. By offering an online course you can help more people design their homes while creating passive income and working less. So you still have time to take 1:1 clients if you wish to.'

Ju De Paula, Design Contestant, Series 1

'If your day job involves having strong organisational skills, that can really help you become a successful designer. If you can plan and manage a project, then you're all good to get going. The great thing about interior design is that it can be structured and about things you can make. It's all about being brave and patient.'

Rochelle Dalphinis, Design Contestant, Series 3

'If you're thinking about becoming an interior designer, you probably already are one. There are programs and apps to use to make yourself appear more professional, but I know none of those. If you enjoy pulling spaces together, keep experimenting; find your style and enjoy being playful. Be the rule breaker and don't follow trends, set them.'

Banjo Beale, Design Contestant, Series 3

'In Series 3, Banjo and Amy both made it into the final because they showed me something extra. They mastered teamwork, creative compromise and the art of colour. They also showed me that they understood the importance of narrative. But, most importantly, they showed that they really understand how a space needs to make you feel.'

Michelle Ogundehin

'Good design is about problem solving, not just about making spaces look good. Our homes need to function well and be safe. Whether it's your own home or that of a client, practise listening to problems and offering solutions to improve how the space can function.'

Terian Tilston, Design Contestant, Series 1

'It's never too late to change your career (I'm doing so at 66 years old!) Go with your gut and you can make it happen. I only wish interior design had been a career option for me in 1974, but I've seen it all – from the shag-pile of the '70s to the minimalist noughties. I think there's actually a lot more design freedom now, and I love seeing all the ideas the young designers come up with.'

Peter Anderson, Design Contestant, Series 3

'If you'd like to become a professional interior designer, I say go for it. Being on this TV show helped me find a lost confidence in what I can achieve, and now I've re-found it, I feel like there's nothing I can't do. I recently tried wallpapering for the first time and loved the challenge, which then spurred me on to try some tiling, and it felt amazing. The design process always takes longer than you think, but it's bloody exciting and gets my adrenaline running – some nights my brain is so over-stimulated, I have to keep working to let all the ideas out, but I love it. Take the leap: we are all fabulous.'

Jon Burns, Design Contestant, Series 2

Design contestants

Series one

Nicki Bamford-Bowes

andthentheywentwild.co.uk /
@andthentheywentwild

Jim Biddulph

jimbiddulph.com / @jimbidd

Kyle Broughton-Frew

kbfdesign.co.uk / @kylebroughton_frew

Trish Coggans

Verity Coleman

rascalandroses.co.uk / @rascalandroses

Ju De Paula

bloominghomesociety.com /
@blueberrylivingco

Jerome Gardener

@jeromegardenerhome

Frank Newbold

franknewbold.com / @franknewbold

Cassie Nicholas

Cassienicholas.co.uk / @dighaushizzle

Terian Tilston

teriantilston.com / @teriantilston_
interiordesign

Series Two

Charlotte Beevor

Charlottebeevor.com / @charlottebeevor

Jon Burns

jonathanscottinteriors.co.uk /
@jonathanscottinteriors

Lynsey Ford

lynseyforddesign.co.uk / @lynseyforddesign

Peter Grech

www.thespacemaker.net /
@thespacemaker_interiors

Paul Moneypenny

@moneypennyinteriors

Siobhan Murphy

@Interiorcurve

Barbara Ramani

barbararamaniinteriors.com / @barbara_
ramani_interiors

Micaela Sharp

Micaelasharpdesign.com /
@micaelasharpdesign

Amy Wilson

amywilsoninteriors.co.uk /
@amywilsoninteriors

Mona Wishkahi

monmondesign.com / @monmondesign

Each design contestant from every series of Interior Design Masters has gone on to do wonderful things within the interiors world, from setting up their own interior designer studios and creating online consultancies and courses, to launching their own product lines and finding fame online as content creators. Some have even penned design books of their own. Find out more about their work, products and services via their social accounts and websites, listed below.

Series Three

Peter Anderson
@peterandersondesigns

Paul Andrews
paulalfredandrews.co.uk / @paul.alfred.andrews

Banjo Beale
Banjobeale.co.uk / @banjo.beale

Molly Coath
mocointerior.com / @molly.coath

Rochelle Dalphinis
lunaspotdesign.com / @rochelle_dalphinis

Amy Davies
amydaviesdesign.com / @amydavies_design

Abi Ann Davis
abianndavis.com / @abianndavis

Fran Lee
@fran_lee_creative

Richard O'Gormon
@househomo

Dean Powell
@darklordinterior

Series Four

Monika Charchula
84-square.com / @84_square

Ry Elliott
ryelliott.com /@ryelliott_

Charlotte Fisher
@thehousethatcharlottebuilt

Buse Gurbuz
@betheinterior

Joanne Hardcastle
@hardcastletowers

Peter Irvine
@thewhitehome

Temi Johnson
temijohnson.com / @ahousemadeofbrass

Jack Kinsey
@jacks_chapel

Karl Mok
www.friendsstudio.co / @karlkai.design

Tom Power
tompowerdesign.com / @tompowerdesign

experts and guest judges

Michelle Ogundehin - Michelleogundehin.com / @michelleogundehin
A trained architect and former Editor-in-Chief of Elle Decoration UK, Michelle is an internationally renowned expert on all things interiors, and has presented Interior Design Masters from its inception. Her first book, *Happy Inside* (Ebury Press, 2020) builds on her interest in how we can harness the power of our homes to improve our mental and physical health.

Matthew Williamson, Interior and product designer, and guest judge
matthewwilliamson.com
@matthewwilliamson
Famed for his love of jewel tones and vibrant nature-influenced patterns, his 'Deya Meadow' wallpaper (available via Osbourne & Little) appears as a backdrop in Michelle's design studio (Series 3), and he has also collaborated with design contestant Cassie Nicholas (Series 1) on a range of bespoke and curated vintage home accessories.

Abigail Ahern, Interior and product designer, and guest judge
Abigailahern.com / @abigailahern
The pioneer of bringing dark décor to the mainstream, Abigail's eponymous shop sells furniture, accessories, faux plants and paints in her trademark inky hues and textural styles. deep-toned, moody style. The author of several books, her latest tomb, *Masterclass* (Pavilion, 2022) shares her personal style secrets behind her aesthetic.

Laurence Llewelyn-Bowen, Interior and product designer, and guest judge
LLB.co.uk / @llewelynbowen
The King of maximalism, Laurence has worked on countless TV makeover shows since the 1990s, including Changing Rooms and HomeFront. A classically trained fine artist, his

flamboyant prints and patterns are available on wallpapers and soft furnishings. His latest book, *More More More* (DK, 2022) offers an ode to decorating in a maximalist style.

Mary Portas, Retail expert and guest judge
Weareportas.com / @maryportasofficial
An expert in retail and passionate about supporting small local businesses and helping boost the British High Street, Mary's podcast series, Beautiful Misfits, and latest book, *Rebuild: How to thrive in the new kindness economy* (Transworld Publishers Ltd, 2021) look at ways to shop and consume in a more mindful way.

Sophie Robinson, Interior design and colour expert, and guest judge
Sophierobinson.co.uk
@sophierobinsoninteriors
A champion of using bold, bright colours in your home (and an expert in the psychology behind them), Sophie offers ever-popular online courses and workshops via her website, and co-hosts The Great Indoors podcast with fellow interiors expert Kate Watson-Smyth.

Guy Oliver, Principal designer/owner at Oliver Laws Ltd and guest judge
Oliverlaws.com / @guyoliver_
Royal Navy Officer turned interior designer, Guy's Masters degree in Architectural and

Design History has led him to specialise in consulting and design work for many historical and listed properties, including Claridge's Hotel and 10 Downing Street.

Linda Boronkay, Interior designer and guest judge
Lindaboronkay.com / @lindaboronkay
Formerly the Design Director of Soho House, Linda's multi-disciplinary design studio is driven by her desire to incorporate integrity and character into her interiors schemes, valuing the emotional impact of design as highly as the aesthetic.

Kit Kemp MBE, Interior and textile designer, and guest judge
Kitkemp.com / @kitkempdesignthread
Founder and Creative Director of Firmdale Hotels, Kit also runs her own design studio specialising in textiles and homeware, and is revered for her artful colour mixing and pattern clashing (fans of her hotel design can buy her furniture, textiles and accessories via her website). Learn more about her processes in her book *Design Secrets* (Hardie Grant, 2021).

Naomi Cleaver, Interior designer and guest judge - **Naomicleaver.com @naomicleaverdesigns**
With extensive experience in the interiors field and appearances on multiple TV design shows, Naomi co-authored the book *All Together Now: The co-living and co-working revolution* (RIBA Publishing, 2021) to highlight how good design can help facilitate hybrid live/work homes and spaces.

Jonathan Adler, Interior and product designer, potter, and guest judge
Jonathanadler.com / @jonathanadler
Famed for his statement 'modern American glamour' aesthetic and his always-playful, sometimes-cheeky range of furniture and accessories, Jonathan's success has spanned the globe and he is sought-after for his style insights and design services worldwide. He has also penned two books, sharing ideas on how to design a home for happiness.

Shayne Brady, Director at Brady Williams, and guest judge - **Bradywilliamsstudio.com / @bradywilliamsresidential**
Heading up the hospitality division of his interior architecture and design studio (his co-director Emily Williams manages the residential design side), they have worked for clients including Harrods, Berkeley Homes and Mandarin Oriental, and featured in various publications for their sumptuously detailed spaces.

Experts from other industries

Sarah Willingham, Entrepreneur and investor - sarahwillingham.com @sarahwillingham

Ross Bailey, CEO at Appear Here - appearhere.co.uk / @appearherehq

Nisha Katona, Restaurateur, author and presenter - nishakatona.com

Jade Jagger, Jewellery designer - jadejagger.co.uk / @jadejezebeljagger

Thomasina Miers, Cook, writer and restaurateur - thomasinamiers.com @thomasinamiers

Index

resources and recommendations

Some product ideas and shopping suggestions to help you recreate what you've seen in the show (and read in this book).

Shop the show

+   Been eyeing up the wallpaper used to decorate Michelle's office and the design hub? The bold floral mural seen in Series 2 is the Deya Meadow (designed by guest judge Matthew Williamson), while the bold monochrome pattern in Series 3 is the Kutani vinyl, both at osborneandlittle.com.

+   Interested in some of the wall murals featured on the show? Bland-design.co.uk created pieces for Siobhan in Series 2 and Banjo in Series 3, which they now sell versions of on their website, while Lynsey's Series 2 mural, featured in her restaurant space, was by artist juliaogden.com.

+   Good news for fans of Amy's numerous bespoke wallpapers featured in her Series 3 designs - she is now selling them via her website, amydaviesdesign.com.

+   Feel like you need Rochelle (Series 3)'s mantra, 'mould to gold' in your life? Then purchase one of her tote bags, which are emblazoned with it (in gold font, of course) via lunaspotdesign.com

+   Their styles may be wildly different, but upcycling queens Abi Ann (Series 3) and Monika (Series 4) both sell their bespoke customisations via abianndavis.com and 84-square.com respectively

+   Series 2 design contestants Micaela and Charlotte have gone on to collaborate on their new venture studiojanettie.com, offering bespoke upholstered furniture and homewares, which combines their talents for print design and upholstery.

+   Love a bold, blocky wall mural but don't fancy painting your own? Richard Gormon (Series 3) has collaborated with wallpaper brand lusthome.com to create a customisable wall mural in his trademark retro-futurism style.

+   Want some more behind-the-scenes rather than buys? Give The TV Carpenter podcast a listen: hosted by one of the shows on-screen carpenters, Wayne Perrey, it features interviews from many interiors experts, including some guest judges and design contestants from the show. Find it via thetvcarpenter.com.

Creative customisations

+ Got something to hide (or after a decorative wall panel)? Order custom fretwork decorative panels from **screenwithenvy.co.uk** (as used in Amy's showhome bedroom in Series 2, episode 1.) On a smaller scale, Charlotte used paintable contemporary 3D moulded panelling in her Series 2 schemes, from **oracdecor.com**.

+ For intricate cornicing or on-trend bobbin mouldings and fluted wall panelling, look at **decwood.co.uk**; if you'd prefer your panelling to have both retro looks and acoustic properties, try **woodveneerhub.co.uk** (as used by Paul in Series 3).

+ Daunted by designing your own murals? Try stencilling instead - **dizzyduckdesigns.com** has a wide range, or add a subtle strip of pattern with a wallpaper border (visit **susieatkinson.com** and **tessnewall.com**).

+ If you're after a bespoke furniture option but don't want to DIY and can't GSI, Tyklo allows you to customise your size requirements for shelving and storage as part of your order (**tyklo.com**). Similarly, to refresh rather than replace fitted cupboards, order your preferred colours and designs online from **customfronts.co.uk** or **plykea.com**.

+ Ditch the paint brush and use coloured or decorative vinyl film for an instant stick-on refresh -check out **architextural.co.uk** and **coverstyl.com** for a vast range of finishes, or for decorative window frosting film, look at **Purlfrost.com**. **d-c-home.com** share lots of step-by-step how-to's using their vinyls, if you need a little inspo.

Upgraded basics

+ For colourful sockets and switches, check out **swtch.co.uk** - or for a more industrial look, try **dowsingandreynolds.com**. Go to **dykeanddean.com** for lighting hardware like ceiling cord hooks, fabric cables and bulb holders.

+ Transform a basic tabletop, desk or console with chic new legs or upgraded furniture feet - **thehairpinlegcompany.co.uk** has a wide range in various colours and styles that can be screwed into place where you want them, or for a DIY-free option, go to **tiptoe.fr/en** - their range of legs incorporates a built-in clamp, instead.

+ Got some specific lighting requirements? **Industville.co.uk** and **hollowaysofludlow.com** both have a broad, on-trend selection of light fittings for specialist areas like bathrooms and gardens. If power points are a problem, invest in chic cordless portable lamps from **humblelights.com** or search **amazon.co.uk** for a 'smart' or 'magic' LED bulb, which are operated by remote control or Bluetooth rather than cable-powered electrics.

Decorating brands to know

Paint

+ Take the stress out of paint shopping by ordering online - brands like **coatpaints.com** and **lick.com** offer stick-on colour samples, to save messing about with tester pots.

+ After a textural, rustic look? Opt for lime wash: **bauwerk.com** has a stunning range (including a palette by guest judge Abigail Ahern).

+ Want to create a bespoke paint colour to perfectly match your favourite art or accessory? **Dulux.co.uk** supplies this service across various finishes - search online for your nearest retailer which uses their paint mixing machine. **Valsparpaint.co.uk** offers a similar service at B&Q stores.

+ Chalk paint isn't just for creating aged effects - it can also be surprisingly durable on difficult surfaces like metal, melamine and even uPVC windows. **Anniesloan.co.uk** and **frenchicpaint.co.uk** both offer reputable ranges.

+ If you like the idea of choosing colours to enhance certain moods but still feel daunted, **Yescolours.com** specialises in feel-good paint hues, curated into collections based on the emotions they evoke.

Wallpaper

+ For blow-the-budget, show-stopping designs, try shopping with British stalwarts such as **cole-and-son.com** and **gpjbaker.com**, while **grahambrown.com** and **scionliving.com** offer more mid-range prices.

+ After more of a bargain? There's great ranges to be found at discount retailers like **bmstores.co.uk** and **wilko.com**, or check out **wallpaperdirect.com** for a wide range of pricepoints from various brands.

+ If you're in the market for a mural, check out the trend-led range at **hovia.com**, or for historical prints and patterns, **surfaceview.co.uk** hold a highly customisable selection. **Feathr.com** holds a unique collection of designs from a range of independent artists, including removable peel-and-stick options as well as standard papers and murals.

+ Get creative and decorate walls with Washi tape instead of wallpaper: **mtmaskingtape.co.uk** have a 'for home' range of wider coloured tape you can use to create coloured bands, while **misopaper.co.uk** stock a vast selection of designs that could be used to add decorative flourishes to bare walls.

+ Wall stickers aren't just for kids - they can offer a creative way to create a bespoke wall pattern. Have a scrawl through **etsy.com** and **notonthehighstreet.com** for a range of spots, shapes and other motifs (these sites are filled with the work of many independent designer-makers, so hold lots of other goodies, too).